SCIENCE FUSION

Lab Manual
Module D

HOLT McDOUGAL

 HOUGHTON MIFFLIN HARCOURT

Acknowledgements for Covers

Cover Photo Credits

Rice fields (bg) ©Keren Su/Corbis; *false color X-rays on hand* (l) ©Lester Lefkowitz/Getty Images; *primate* (cl) ©Bruno Morandi/The Image Bank/Getty Images; *red cells* (cr) ©Todd Davidson/Getty Images; *fossils* (r) ©Yoshihi Tanaka/amana images/Getty Images

Printed in the U.S.A.

ISBN   978-0-547-59266-4

3 4 5 6 7 8 9 10   0982   20 19 18 17 16 15 14 13 12
4500364970   A B C D E F G

Contents

Using Your *ScienceFusion* Lab Program

Your *ScienceFusion* Lab Program is designed to include activities that address a variety of student levels, inquiry levels, time availability, and materials. In this Lab Manual, you will find that each student activity is preceded by Teacher Resources with valuable information about the activity.

Activity Type: Quick Lab

Each lesson within each unit is supported by two to three short activities called Quick Labs. Quick Labs involve simple materials and set-up. The student portion of each Quick Lab should take less than 30 minutes. Each Quick Lab includes Teacher Resources and one Student Datasheet.

Activity Types: Exploration Lab, Field Lab, and S.T.E.M. Lab

Each unit is supported by one to four additional labs that require one or more class periods to complete. Each Exploration, Field, and S.T.E.M. Lab includes Teacher Resources and two Student Datasheets. Each Student Datasheet is targeted to address different inquiry levels. Below is a description of each lab:

- **Exploration Labs** are traditional lab activities. The labs are designed to be conducted with standard laboratory equipment and materials.
- **Field Labs** are lab activities that are partially or completely performed outside the classroom or laboratory.
- **S.T.E.M. Labs** are lab activities that focus on Science, Technology, Engineering, and Math skills.

Inquiry Level

The inquiry level of each activity indicates the level at which students direct the activity. An activity that is entirely student-directed is often called Open Inquiry or Independent Inquiry. True Open or Independent Inquiry is based on a question posed by students, uses experimental processes designed by students, and requires students to find the connections between data and content. These types of activities result from student interest in the world around them. The *ScienceFusion* Lab Program provides activities that allow for a wide variety of student involvement.

- DIRECTED **Inquiry** is the least student-directed of the inquiry levels. Directed Inquiry activities provide students with an introduction to content, a procedure to follow, and direction on how to organize and analyze data.
- GUIDED **Inquiry** indicates that an activity is moderately student-directed. Guided Inquiry activities require students to select materials, procedural steps, data analysis techniques, or other aspects of the activity.
- INDEPENDENT **Inquiry** indicates that an activity is highly student-directed. Though students are provided with ideas, partial procedures, or suggestions, they are responsible for selecting many aspects of the activity.

Each Quick Lab includes one Student Datasheet that is written to support the inquiry level indicated on the Teacher Resources. Each Exploration Lab, Field Lab, and S.T.E.M. Lab includes two Student Datasheets, each written to support an inquiry level. In addition, the Teacher Resources includes one or more modification suggestions to adjust the inquiry level.

Student Level

The *ScienceFusion* Lab Program is designed to provide successful experiences for all levels of students.

- **BASIC** activities focus on introductory content and concepts taught in the lesson. These activities can be used with any level of student, including those who may have learning or language difficulties, but they may not provide a challenge for advanced students.
- **GENERAL** activities are appropriate for most students.
- **ADVANCED** activities require good understanding of the content and concepts in the lesson or ask students to manipulate content to arrive at the learning objective. Advanced activities may provide a challenge to advanced students, but they may be difficult for average or basic-level students.

Lab Ratings

Each activity is rated on three criteria to provide you with information that you may find useful when determining if an activity is appropriate for your resources.

- **Teacher Prep** rating indicates the amount of preparation you will need to provide before students can perform the activity.
- **Student Setup** rating indicates the amount of preparation students will need to perform before they begin to collect data.
- **Cleanup** rating indicates the amount of effort required to dispose of materials and disassemble the set-up of the activity.

Teacher Notes

Information and background that may be helpful to you can be found in the Teacher Notes section of the Teacher Resources. The information includes hints and a list of skills that students will practice during the activity.

Science Kit

Hands-on materials needed to complete all the labs in the Lab Manual for each module have been conveniently configured into consumable and non-consumable kits. Common materials provided by parents or your school/district are not included in the kits. Laboratory equipment commonly found in most schools has been separately packaged in a Grades 6–8 Inquiry Equipment Kit. This economical option allows schools to buy equipment only if they need it and can be shared among teachers and across grade levels. For more information on the material kits or to order, contact your local Holt McDougal sales representative or call customer service at 800-462-6595.

Online Lab Resources

The *ScienceFusion* Lab Program offers many additional resources online through our web site thinkcentral.com. These resources include:

Teacher Notes, Transparencies, and **Copymasters** are found in the Online Toolkit. Student-friendly tutorial Transparencies are available to print as transparencies or handouts. Each set of Transparencies is supported by Teacher Notes that include background information, teaching tips, and techniques. Teacher Notes, Transparencies, and Copymatsters are available to teach a broad range of skills.

- **Modeling Experimental Design** Teacher Notes and Transparencies cover Scientific Methods skills, such as Making Qualitative Observations, Developing a Hypothesis, and Making Valid Inferences.

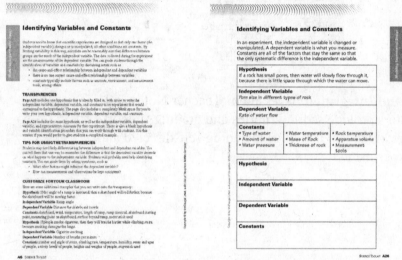

- **Writing in the Sciences** Teacher Notes and Transparencies teach written communication skills, such as Writing a Lab Report and Maintaining a Science Notebook. In addition, the Lab Report Template provides a structured format that students can use as the basis for their own lab reports.

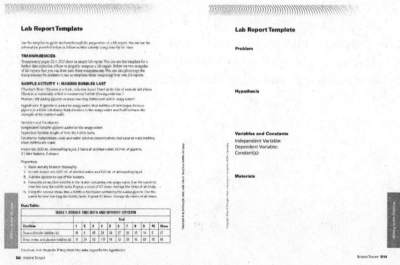

- **Math in Science Tools** Teacher Notes and Transparencies teach the math skills that are needed for data analysis in labs. These Teacher Notes and Transparencies support the S.T.E.M. concepts found throughout the *ScienceFusion* program.

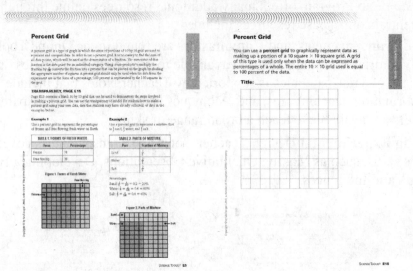

- **Rubrics and Integrated Assessment** Teacher Notes and Copymasters provide scoring rubrics and grading support for a range of student activities including self-directed and guided experiments.

- **Planning for Science Fairs and Competitions** Teacher Notes and Copymasters provide planning and preparation techniques for science fairs and other competitions.

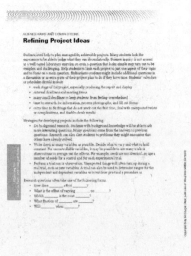

Making Your Laboratory a Safe Place

Concern for safety must begin before any activity in the classroom and before students enter the lab. A careful review of the facilities should be a basic part of preparation for each school term. You should investigate the physical environment, identify any safety risks, and inspect your work areas for compliance with safety regulations.

The review of the lab should be thorough, and all safety issues must be addressed immediately. Keep a file of your review, and add to the list each year. This will allow you to continue to raise the standard of safety in your lab and classroom.

Many classroom experiments, demonstrations, and other activities are classics that have been used for years. This familiarity may lead to a comfort that can obscure inherent safety concerns. Review all experiments, demonstrations, and activities for safety concerns before presenting them to the class. Identify and eliminate potential safety hazards.

1. **Identify the Risks** Before introducing any activity, demonstration, or experiment to the class, analyze it and consider what could possibly go wrong. Carefully review the list of materials to make sure they are safe. Inspect the equipment in your lab or classroom to make sure it is in good working order. Read the procedures to make sure they are safe. Record any hazards or concerns you identify.

2. **Evaluate the Risks** Minimize the risks you identified in the last step without sacrificing learning. Remember that no activity you perform in the lab or classroom is worth risking injury. Thus, extremely hazardous activities, or those that violate your school's policies, must be eliminated. For activities that present smaller risks, analyze each risk carefully to determine its likelihood. If the pedagogical value of the activity does not outweigh the risks, the activity must be eliminated.

3. **Select Controls to Address Risks** Even low-risk activities require controls to eliminate or minimize the risks. Make sure that in devising controls you do not substitute an equally or more hazardous alternative. Some control methods include the following:

   - Explicit verbal and written warnings may be added or posted.
   - Equipment may be rebuilt or relocated, parts may be replaced, or equipment be replaced entirely by safer alternatives.
   - Risky procedures may be eliminated.
   - Activities may be changed from student activities to teacher demonstrations.

4. **Implement and Review Selected Controls** Controls do not help if they are forgotten or not enforced. The implementation and review of controls should be as systematic and thorough as the initial analysis of safety concerns in the lab and laboratory activities.

Safety with Chemicals

Label student reagent containers with the substance's name and hazard class(es) (flammable, reactive, etc.). Dispose of hazardous waste chemicals according to federal, state, and local regulations. Refer to the MSDS for recommended disposal procedures. Remove all sources of flames, sparks, and heat from the laboratory when any flammable material is being used.

Material Safety Data Sheets

The purpose of a Material Safety Data Sheet (MSDS) is to provide readily accessible information on chemical substances commonly used in the science laboratory or in industry. The MSDS should be kept on file and referred to BEFORE handling ANY chemical. The MSDS can also be used to instruct students on chemical hazards, to evaluate spill and disposal procedures, and to warn of incompatibility with other chemicals or mixtures.

Storing Chemicals

Never store chemicals alphabetically, as this greatly increases the risk of promoting a violent reaction.

Storage Suggestions

1. Always lock the storeroom and all its cabinets when not in use.
2. Students should not be allowed in the storeroom and preparation area.
3. Avoid storing chemicals on the floor of the storeroom.
4. Do not store chemicals above eye level or on the top shelf in the storeroom.
5. Be sure shelf assemblies are firmly secured to the walls.
6. Provide anti-roll lips on all shelves.
7. Shelving should be constructed out of wood. Metal cabinets and shelves are easily corroded.
8. Avoid metal, adjustable shelf supports and clips. They can corrode, causing shelves to collapse.
9. Acids, flammables, poisons, and oxidizers should each be stored in their own locking storage cabinet.

Safety with Animals

It is recommended that teachers follow the NABT Position Statement "The Use of Animals in Biology Education" issued by the National Association of Biology Teachers (available at www.nabt.org).

Safety In Handling Preserved Materials

The following practices are recommended when handling preserved specimens:

1. NEVER dissect road-kills or nonpreserved slaughterhouse materials.
2. Wear protective gloves and splash-proof safety goggles at all times when handling preserving fluids and preserved specimens and during dissection.
3. Wear lab aprons. Use of an old shirt or smock under the lab apron is recommended.
4. Conduct dissection activities in a well-ventilated area.
5. Do not allow preservation or body-cavity fluids to contact skin. Fixatives do not distinguish between living or dead tissues. Biological supply firms may use formalin-based fixatives of varying concentrations to initially fix zoological and botanical specimens. Some provide specimens that are freezedried and rehydrated in a 10% isopropyl alcohol solution. Many suppliers provide fixed botanical materials in 50% glycerin.

Reduction Of Free Formaldehyde

Currently, federal regulations mandate a permissible exposure level of 0.75 ppm for formaldehyde. Contact your supplier for Material Data Safety Sheet (MSDS) that details the amount of formaldehyde present as well as gas-emitting characteristics for individual specimens. Prewash specimens (in a loosely covered container) in running tap water for 1–4 hours to dilute the fixative. Formaldehyde may also be chemically bound (thereby reducing danger) by immersing washed specimens in a 0.5–1.0% potassium bisulfate solution overnight or by placing them in 1% phenoxyethanol holding solutions.

Safety with Microbes

WHAT YOU CAN'T SEE CAN HURT YOU

Pathogenic (disease-causing) microorganisms are not appropriate investigation tools in the high school laboratory and should never be used.

Consult with the school nurse to screen students whose immune systems may be compromised by illness or who may be receiving immunosuppressive drug therapy. Such individuals are extraordinarily sensitive to potential infection from generally harmless microorganisms and should not participate in laboratory activities unless permitted to do so by a physician. Do not allow students who have any open cuts, abrasions, or open sores to work with microorganisms.

HOW TO USE ASEPTIC TECHNIQUE

- Demonstrate correct aseptic technique to students prior to conducting a lab activity. Never pipet liquid media by mouth. When possible, use sterile cotton applicator sticks instead of inoculating loops and Bunsen burner flames for culture inoculation. Remember to use appropriate precautions when disposing of cotton applicator sticks: they should be autoclaved or sterilized before disposal.

- Treat all microbes as pathogenic. Seal with tape all petri dishes containing bacterial cultures. Do not use blood agar plates, and never attempt to cultivate microbes from a human or animal source.

- Never dispose of microbe cultures without sterilizing them first. Autoclave or steam-sterilize at 120°C and 15 psi for 15 to 20 minutes all used cultures and any materials that have come in contact with them. If these devices are not available, flood or immerse these articles in full-strength household bleach for 30 minutes, and then discard. Use the autoclave or steam sterilizer yourself; do not allow students to use these devices.

- Wash all lab surfaces with a disinfectant solution before and after handling bacterial cultures.

HOW TO HANDLE BACTERIOLOGICAL SPILLS

- Never allow students to clean up bacteriological spills. Keep on hand a spill kit containing 500 mL of full-strength household bleach, biohazard bags (autoclavable), forceps, and paper towels.

- In the event of a bacterial spill, cover the area with a layer of paper towels. Wet the paper towels with bleach, and allow them to stand for 15 to 20 minutes. Wearing gloves and using forceps, place the residue in the biohazard bag. If broken glass is present, use a brush and dustpan to collect material, and place it in a suitably marked puncture-resistant container for disposal.

Personal Protective Equipment

Chemical goggles (Meeting ANSI Standard Z87.1) These should be worn with any chemical or chemical solution other than water, when heating substances, using any mechanical device, or observing physical processes that could eject an object.

Face shield (Meeting ANSI Standard Z87.1) Use in combination with eye goggles when working with corrosives.

Contact lenses The wearing of contact lenses for cosmetic reasons should be prohibited in the laboratory. If a student must wear contact lenses prescribed by a physician, that student should be instructed to wear eye-cup safety goggles, similar to swimmer's cup goggles, meeting ANSI Standard Z87.1.

Eye-wash station The device must be capable of delivering a copious, gentle flow of water to both eyes for at least 15 minutes. Portable liquid supply devices are not satisfactory and should not be used. A plumbed-in fixture or a perforated spray head on the end of a hose attached to a plumbed-in outlet is suitable if it is designed for use as an eye-wash fountain and meets ANSI Standard Z358.1. It must be within a 30-second walking distance from any spot in the room.

Safety shower (Meeting ANSI Standard Z358.1) Location should be within a 30-second walking distance from any spot in the room. Students should be instructed in the use of the safety shower in the event of a fire or chemical splash on their body that cannot simply be washed off.

Gloves Polyethylene, neoprene rubber, or disposable plastic may be used. Nitrile or butyl rubber gloves are recommended when handling corrosives.

Apron Rubber-coated cloth or vinyl (nylon-coated) halter is recommended.

Student Safety in the Laboratory

Systematic, careful lab work is an essential part of any science program. The equipment and apparatus students will use present various safety hazards. You must be aware of these hazards before students engage in any lab activity. The Teacher Resource Pages at the beginning of each lab in this Lab Manual will guide you in properly directing the equipment use during the experiments. Photocopy the information on the following pages for students. These safety rules always apply in the lab and in the field.

Safety Symbols

The following safety symbols will appear in the instructions for labs and activities to emphasize important notes of caution. Learn what they represent so that you can take the appropriate precautions.

Eye Protection
- Wear approved safety goggles at all times in the lab as directed.
- If chemicals get into your eyes, flush your eyes immediately.
- Do not wear contact lenses in the lab.
- Do not look directly at the sun or any intense light source or laser.

Hand Safety
- Do not cut an object while holding the object in your hand.
- Wear appropriate protective gloves when working with an open flame, chemicals, solutions, or wild or unknown plants.
- Use a heat-resistant mitt to handle equipment that may be hot.

Clothing Protection
- Wear an apron or lab coat at all times in the lab.
- Tie back long hair, secure loose clothing, and remove loose jewelry so that they do not knock over equipment, get caught in moving parts, or come into contact with hazardous materials or electrical connections.
- Do not wear open-toed shoes, sandals, or canvas shoes in the lab.
- When outside for lab, wear long sleeves, long pants, socks, and closed shoes.

Glassware Safety
- Inspect glassware before use; do not use chipped or cracked glassware.
- Use heat-resistant glassware for heating materials or storing hot liquids.
- Notify your teacher immediately if a piece of glassware or a light bulb breaks.

Sharp-Object Safety
- Use extreme care when handling all sharp and pointed instruments.
- Cut objects on a suitable surface, always in a direction away from your body.
- Be aware of sharp objects or edges on equipment or apparatus.

Chemical Safety
- If a chemical gets on your skin, on your clothing, or in your eyes, rinse it immediately (shower, faucet or eyewash fountain) and alert your teacher.
- Do not clean up spilled chemicals yourself unless your teacher directs you to do so.
- Do not inhale any gas or vapor unless your teacher directs you to do so.
- Handle materials that emit vapors or gases in a well-ventilated area.

Safety Symbols continued

	Electrical Safety • Do not use equipment with frayed electrical cords or loose plugs. • Fasten electrical cords to work surfaces by using tape. • Do not use electrical equipment near water or when clothing or hands are wet. • Hold the plug housing when you plug in or unplug equipment. • Be aware that wire coils in electrical circuits may heat up rapidly.
	Heating Safety • Be aware of any source of flames, sparks, or heat (such as open flames, heating coils, or hot plates) before working with any flammable substances. • Avoid using open flames. • Know the location of lab fire extinguishers and fire-safety blankets. • Know your school's fire-evacuation routes. • If your clothing catches on fire, walk to the lab shower to put out the fire. • Never leave a hot plate unattended while it is turned on or while it is cooling. • Use tongs or appropriate insulated holders when handling heated objects. • Allow all equipment to cool before storing it.
	Plant Safety • Do not eat any part of a plant or plant seed. • When outside, do not pick any wild plants unless your teacher instructs you to do so. • Wash your hands thoroughly after handling any part of a plant.
	Animal Safety • Handle animals only as your teacher directs. • Treat animals carefully and respectfully. • Wash your hands thoroughly after handling any animal.
	Proper Waste Disposal • Clean and sanitize all work surfaces and personal protective equipment after each lab period as directed by your teacher. • Dispose of hazardous materials only as directed by your teacher. • Dispose of sharp objects (such as broken glass) in the appropriate sharps or broken glass container as directed by your teacher.
	Hygienic Care • Keep your hands away from your face while you are working on any activity. • Wash your hands thoroughly before you leave the lab or after any activity. • Remove contaminated clothing immediately.

Safety in the Laboratory

1. **Always wear a lab apron and safety goggles.** Wear these safety devices whenever you are in the lab, not just when you are working on an experiment.

2. **No contact lenses in the lab.** Contact lenses should not be worn during any investigations in which you are using chemicals (even if you are wearing goggles). In the event of an accident, chemicals can get behind contact lenses and cause serious damage before the lenses can be removed. If your doctor requires that you wear contact lenses instead of glasses, you should wear eye-cup safety goggles in the lab. Ask your doctor or your teacher how to use this very important and special eye protection.

3. **Personal apparel should be appropriate for laboratory work.** On lab days, avoid wearing long necklaces, dangling bracelets, bulky jewelry, and bulky or loose-fitting clothing. Long hair should be tied back. Loose, flopping, or dangling items may get caught in moving parts, accidentally contact electrical connections, or interfere with the investigation in some potentially hazardous manner. In addition, chemical fumes may react with some jewelry, such as pearls, and ruin them. Cotton clothing is preferable to wool, nylon, or polyesters. Wear shoes that will protect your feet from chemical spills and falling objects— no open-toed shoes or sandals and no shoes with woven leather straps.

4. **NEVER work alone in the laboratory.** Work in the lab only while supervised by your teacher. Do not leave equipment unattended while it is in operation.

5. **Only books and notebooks needed for the activity should be in the lab.** Only the lab notebook and perhaps the textbook should be used. Keep other books, backpacks, purses, and similar items in your desk, locker, or designated storage area.

6. **Read the entire activity before entering the lab.** Your teacher will review any applicable safety precautions before you begin the lab activity. If you are not sure of something, ask your teacher about it.

7. Always heed safety symbols and cautions in the instructions for the experiments, in handouts, and on posters in the room, and always heed cautions given verbally by your teacher. They are provided for your safety.

8. Know the proper fire drill procedures and the locations of fire exits and emergency equipment. Make sure you know the procedures to follow in case of a fire or other emergency.

9. **If your clothing catches on fire, do not run;** WALK to the safety shower, stand under the showerhead, and turn the water on. Call to your teacher while you do this.

10. **Report all accidents to the teacher** IMMEDIATELY, no matter how minor. In addition, if you get a headache or feel ill or dizzy, tell your teacher immediately.

11. **Report all spills to your teacher immediately.** Call your teacher, rather than cleaning a spill yourself. Your teacher will tell you if it is safe for you to clean up the spill. If it is not safe for you to clean up the spill, your teacher will know how the spill should be cleaned up safely.

12. If a lab directs you to design your own experiments, procedures must be approved by your teacher BEFORE you begin work.

13. DO NOT perform unauthorized experiments or use equipment or apparatus in a manner for which they were not intended. Use only materials and equipment listed in the activity equipment list or authorized by your teacher. Steps in a procedure should only be performed as described in the lab manual or as approved by your teacher.

14. **Stay alert while in the lab, and proceed with caution.** Be aware of others near you or your equipment when you are proceeding with the experiment. If you are not sure of how to proceed, ask your teacher for help.

15. **Horseplay in the lab is very dangerous.** Laboratory equipment and apparatus are not toys; never play in the lab or use lab time or equipment for anything other than their intended purpose.

16. Food, beverages, and chewing gum are NEVER permitted in the laboratory.

17. **NEVER taste chemicals.** Do not touch chemicals or allow them to contact areas of bare skin.

18. **Use extreme CAUTION when working with hot plates or other heating devices.** Keep your head, hands, hair, and clothing away from the flame or heating area, and turn the devices off when they are not in use. Remember that metal surfaces connected to the heated area will become hot by conduction. Gas burners should be lit only with a spark lighter. Make sure all heating devices and gas valves are turned off before leaving the laboratory. Never leave a hot plate or other heating device unattended when it is in use. Remember that many metal, ceramic, and glass items do not always look hot when they are heated. Allow all items to cool before storing them.

19. **Exercise caution when working with electrical equipment.** Do not use electrical equipment that has frayed or twisted wires. Be sure your hands are dry before you use electrical equipment. Do not let electrical cords dangle from work stations; dangling cords can cause tripping or electrical shocks.

20. **Keep work areas and apparatus clean and neat.** Always clean up any clutter made during the course of lab work, rearrange apparatus in an orderly manner, and report any damaged or missing items.

21. Always thoroughly wash your hands with soap and water at the conclusion of each investigation.

Safety in the Field

Activities conducted outdoors require some advance planning to ensure a safe environment. The following general guidelines should be followed for fieldwork.

1. **Know your mission.** Your teacher will tell you the goal of the field trip in advance. Be sure to have your permission slip approved before the trip, and check to be sure that you have all necessary supplies for the day's activity.

2. **Find out about on-site hazards before setting out.** Determine whether poisonous plants or dangerous animals are likely to be present where you are going. Know how to identify these hazards. Find out about other hazards, such as steep or slippery terrain.

3. **Wear protective clothing.** Dress in a manner that will keep you warm, comfortable, and dry. Decide in advance whether you will need sunglasses, a hat, gloves, boots, or rain gear to suit the terrain and local weather conditions.

4. **Do not approach or touch wild animals.** If you see a threatening animal, call your teacher immediately. Avoid any living thing that may sting, bite, scratch, or otherwise cause injury.

5. **Do not touch wild plants or pick wildflowers unless specifically instructed to do so by your teacher.** Many wild plants can be irritating or toxic. Never taste any wild plant.

6. **Do not wander away from others.** Travel with a partner at all times. Stay within an area where you can be seen or heard in case you run into trouble.

7. **Report all hazards or accidents to your teacher immediately.** Even if the incident seems unimportant, let your teacher know what happened.

8. **Maintain the safety of the environment.** Do not remove anything from the field site without your teacher's permission. Stay on trails, when possible, to avoid trampling delicate vegetation. Never leave garbage behind at a field site. Leave natural areas as you found them.

Laboratory Techniques

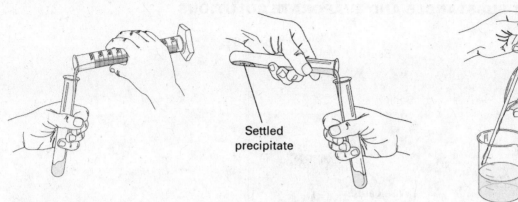

Settled precipitate

Figure A   **Figure B**   **Figure C**

HOW TO DECANT AND TRANSFER LIQUIDS

1. The safest way to transfer a liquid from a graduated cylinder to a test tube is shown in **Figure** A. The liquid is transferred at arm's length, with the elbows slightly bent. This position enables you to see what you are doing while maintaining steady control of the equipment.

2. Sometimes, liquids contain particles of insoluble solids that sink to the bottom of a test tube or beaker. Use one of the methods shown above to separate a supernatant (the clear fluid) from insoluble solids.

   a. **Figure B** shows the proper method of decanting a supernatant liquid from a test tube.

   b. **Figure C** shows the proper method of decanting a supernatant liquid from a beaker by using a stirring rod. The rod should touch the wall of the receiving container. Hold the stirring rod against the lip of the beaker containing the supernatant. As you pour, the liquid will run down the rod and fall into the beaker resting below. When you use this method, the liquid will not run down the side of the beaker from which you are pouring.

Laboratory Techniques continued

HOW TO HEAT SUBSTANCES AND EVAPORATE SOLUTIONS

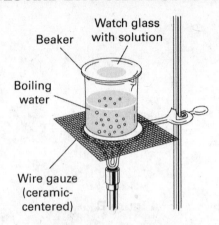

FIGURE D

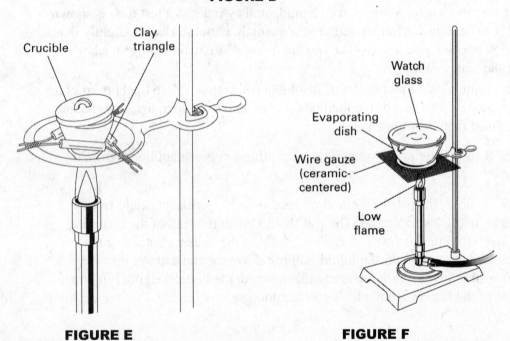

FIGURE E   **FIGURE F**

1. Use care in selecting glassware for high-temperature heating. The glassware should be heat resistant.

2. When heating glassware by using a gas flame, use a ceramic-centered wire gauze to protect glassware from direct contact with the flame. Wire gauzes can withstand extremely high temperatures and will help prevent glassware from breaking. **Figure D** shows the proper setup for evaporating a solution over a water bath.

3. In some experiments, you are required to heat a substance to high temperatures in a porcelain crucible. Figure E shows the proper apparatus setup used to accomplish this task.

4. **Figure F** shows the proper setup for evaporating a solution in a porcelain evaporating dish with a watch glass cover that prevents spattering.

Laboratory Techniques continued

5. Glassware, porcelain, and iron rings that have been heated may look cool after they are removed from a heat source, but these items can still burn your skin even after several minutes of cooling. Use tongs, test-tube holders, or heat-resistant mitts and pads whenever you handle these pieces of apparatus.

6. You can test the temperature of beakers, ring stands, wire gauzes, or other pieces of apparatus that have been heated by holding the back of your hand close to their surfaces before grasping them. You will be able to feel any energy as heat generated from the hot surfaces. DO NOT TOUCH THE APPARATUS. Allow plenty of time for the apparatus to cool before handling.

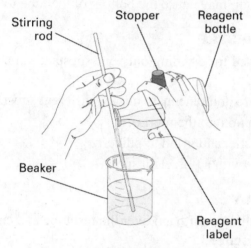

FIGURE G

HOW TO POUR LIQUID FROM A REAGENT BOTTLE

1. Read the label at least three times before using the contents of a reagent bottle.

2. Never lay the stopper of a reagent bottle on the lab table.

3. When pouring a caustic or corrosive liquid into a beaker, use a stirring rod to avoid drips and spills. Hold the stirring rod against the lip of the reagent bottle. Estimate the amount of liquid you need, and pour this amount along the rod, into the beaker. See **Figure G**.

4. Extra precaution should be taken when handling a bottle of acid. Remember the following important rules: Never add water to any concentrated acid, particularly sulfuric acid, because the mixture can splash and will generate a lot of energy as heat. To dilute any acid, add the acid to water in small quantities while stirring slowly. Remember the "triple A's"—*Always Add Acid* to water.

5. Examine the outside of the reagent bottle for any liquid that has dripped down the bottle or spilled on the counter top. Your teacher will show you the proper procedures for cleaning up a chemical spill.

6. Never pour reagents back into stock bottles. At the end of the experiment, your teacher will tell you how to dispose of any excess chemicals.

Laboratory Techniques continued

HOW TO HEAT MATERIAL IN A TEST TUBE

1. Check to see that the test tube is heat resistant.
2. Always use a test tube holder or clamp when heating a test tube.
3. Never point a heated test tube at anyone, because the liquid may splash out of the test tube.
4. Never look down into the test tube while heating it.
5. Heat the test tube from the upper portions of the tube downward, and continuously move the test tube, as shown in **Figure H**. Do not heat any one spot on the test tube. Otherwise, a pressure buildup may cause the bottom of the tube to blow out.

HOW TO USE A MORTAR AND PESTLE

1. A mortar and pestle should be used for grinding only one substance at a time. See **Figure I**.
2. Never use a mortar and pestle for simultaneously mixing different substances.
3. Place the substance to be broken up into the mortar.
4. Pound the substance with the pestle, and grind to pulverize.
5. Remove the powdered substance with a porcelain spoon.

HOW TO DETECT ODORS SAFELY

1. Test for the odor of gases by wafting your hand over the test tube and cautiously sniffing the fumes as shown in **Figure J**.
2. Do not inhale any fumes directly.
3. Use a fume hood whenever poisonous or irritating fumes are present. DO NOT waft and sniff poisonous or irritating fumes.

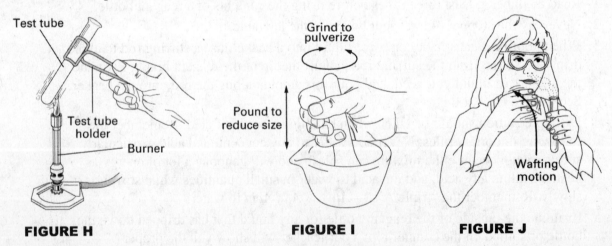

FIGURE H   **FIGURE I**   **FIGURE J**

Student Safety Quiz

Circle the letter of the BEST answer.

1. Before starting an investigation or lab procedure, you should

    a. try an experiment of your own

    b. open all containers and packages

    c. read all directions and make sure you understand them

    d. handle all the equipment to become familiar with it

2. When pouring chemicals between containers, you should hold the containers over

    a. the floor or a waste basket

    b. a fire blanket or an oven mitt

    c. an eyewash station or a water fountain

    d. a sink or your work area

3. If you get hurt or injured in any way, you should

    a. tell your teacher immediately

    b. find bandages or a first aid kit

    c. go to the principal's office

    d. get help after you finish the lab

4. If your glassware is chipped or broken, you should

    a. use it only for solid materials

    b. give it to your teacher

    c. put it back into the storage cabinet

    d. increase the damage so that it is obvious

5. If you have unused chemicals after finishing a procedure, you should

    a. pour them down a sink or drain

    b. mix them all together in a bucket

    c. put them back into their original containers

    d. throw them away where your teacher tells you to

6. If electrical equipment has a frayed cord, you should

   a. unplug the equipment by pulling on the cord

   b. let the cord hang over the side of a counter or table

   c. tell your teacher about the problem immediately

   d. wrap tape around the cord to repair it

7. If you need to determine the odor of a chemical or a solution, you should

   a. use your hand to bring fumes from the container to your nose

   b. bring the container under your nose and inhale deeply

   c. tell your teacher immediately

   d. use odor-sensing equipment

8. When working with materials that might fly into the air and hurt someone's eye, you should wear

   a. goggles

   b. an apron

   c. gloves

   d. a hat

9. Before doing experiments involving a heat source, you should know the location of the

   a. door

   b. windows

   c. fire extinguisher

   d. overhead lights

10. If you get a chemical in your eye, you should

   a. wash your hands immediately

   b. put the lid back on the chemical container

   c. wait to see if your eye becomes irritated

   d. use the eyewash right away

11. When working with a flame or heat source, you should

    a. tie back long hair or hair that hangs in front of your eyes

    b. heat substances or objects inside a closed container

    c. touch an object with your bare hand to see how hot it is

    d. throw hot objects into the trash when you are done with them

12. As you cut with a knife or other sharp instrument, you should move the instrument

    a. toward you

    b. away from you

    c. vertically

    d. horizontally

LAB SAFETY QUIZ

Answer Key

1.	C	5.	D	9.	C
2.	D	6.	C	10.	D
3.	A	7.	A	11.	A
4.	B	8.	A	12.	B

Student Safety Contract

Read carefully the Student Safety Contract below. Then, fill in your name in the first blank, date the contract, and sign it.

Student Safety Contract

I will
- read the lab investigation before coming to class
- wear personal protective equipment as directed to protect my eyes, face, hands, and body while conducting class activities
- follow all instructions given by the teacher
- conduct myself in a responsible manner at all times in a laboratory situation

I, _____, have read and agree to abide by the safety regulations as set forth above and any additional printed instructions provided by my teacher or the school district.

I agree to follow all other written and oral instructions given in class.

Signature: _____

Date: _____

QUICK LAB GUIDED *Inquiry*

Which Abiotic and Biotic Factors Are Found in an Ecosystem? GENERAL

👥 Small groups
🕐 20 minutes

LAB RATINGS

LESS ←————————→ MORE

Teacher Prep —
Student Setup —
Cleanup —

MATERIALS
For each group
- cards, index with habitat descriptions
- pencils, colored (or other drawing tools)
- poster board or construction paper

TEACHER NOTES

In this activity, students will investigate organisms that can be supported by abiotic factors in an ecosystem and will make a poster that reveals their findings. Prepare an index card for each of the following: Arctic tundra near the North Pole; a desert that has very little water; a warm, sunny saltwater environment surrounding an island; a cold coniferous forest that experiences a very short summer; a meadow with a small, shallow pond; and a flooded swamp near the coast. Distribute one card to each group at the beginning of the activity. Possible materials for making the poster include crayons, colored pencils, markers, paints, and magazine photos.

Tip This activity will help students understand how living things are affected by the nonliving things in their environment.

Student Tip Think about the nonliving things around you. All ecosystems contain abiotic factors.

Skills Focus Making Observations, Drawing Conclusions

MODIFICATION FOR INDEPENDENT *Inquiry*

Have students brainstorm ways in which their daily activities affect the environment. Ask them to generate a list of questions that would help them extend and refine their drawings.

My Notes

_____

_____

_____

_____

_____

Answer Key

2. Answers will vary for each ecosystem, but might include sunlight, rain, water, and wind.

3. Answers will vary for each ecosystem, but should include the different organisms living there.

4. Check students' drawings to make sure they include all the abiotic and biotic factors of the ecosystem on the card assigned.

5. Accept all reasonable answers.

6. Accept all reasonable answers; students should demonstrate an understanding of the relationship between an organism and other living things in its environment.

7. Accept all reasonable answers; students should demonstrate an understanding that if an abiotic factor changes, there will be consequences for the organisms living in the ecosystem.

Which Abiotic and Biotic Factors Are Found in an Ecosystem?

In this activity, you will explore the kinds of organisms that live in an ecosystem and how they are affected by the abiotic factors there.

PROCEDURE

1 Read the description of the ecosystem assigned by your teacher.

2 Make a list of the abiotic factors that are part of that ecosystem.

_____

_____

_____

_____

_____

3 Make a list of all the biotic factors that are part of that ecosystem.

_____

_____

_____

_____

_____

_____

4 Use the drawing materials to make a sketch of your ecosystem. Be sure to include all the abiotic factors you listed in Step 2 and the biotic factors from Step 3.

5 Choose one of the organisms from your drawing. What is the relationship between this organism and the abiotic factors in the ecosystem?

_____

_____

_____

_____

OBJECTIVES

- Identify the abiotic and biotic factors in an ecosystem.
- Draw a sketch of an ecosystem.
- Describe the types and variety of organisms that can be supported by the abiotic factors in an ecosystem.

MATERIALS

For each group
- cards, index with habitat descriptions
- pencils, colored (or other drawing tools)
- poster board or construction paper

Quick Lab continued

6 What is the relationship between the organism you chose in Step 5 and the other living things in the ecosystem?

_____

_____

_____

_____

7 Choose one abiotic factor from your drawing that could change over time. Explain how this change would affect the organisms in the ecosystem.

_____

_____

_____

_____

_____

_____

QUICK LAB GUIDED *Inquiry*

Which Biome? GENERAL

👥 Student pairs

🕐 20 minutes

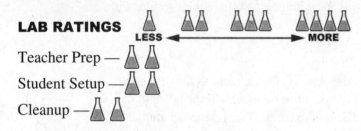

LAB RATINGS

Teacher Prep —

Student Setup —

Cleanup —

MATERIALS

For each pair
- cloth, wool
- cup, plastic with lid (3)
- foam (or other flexible insulating material)
- tape, masking
- thermometers (3)
- water, heated

For each student
- lab apron
- safety goggles

SAFETY INFORMATION

Remind students to review all safety cautions and icons before beginning this lab. Tell students to be careful to avoid spills when handling heated water and to wear protective clothing at all times. Inform students that if any spills occur, they should notify you immediately. Also, instruct students to avoid touching a thermometer if it breaks and to notify you of the breakage. At end end of the activity, have students carefully remove the thermometers and pour the water into a sink.

TEACHER NOTES

In this activity, students will model three different animals, each with a different amount of insulation (i.e., body fat and fur), and determine the appropriate biome for each animal based on the animal's retention of body heat.

Tip Materials required for this lab (as listed later) include a cup and a lid. The hole in the lid needs to be just large enough to fit the thermometer through. If the hole is too large, it can affect the results of this experiment negatively. Make sure that the hole you cut in the lid fits the thermometer snugly. For best results, you may want to cut the holes in the cup lids ahead of time. Water should be heated ahead of time to no more than 60 °C. A thermos can be used to store heated water.

Skills Focus Practicing Lab Techniques, Making Inferences, Designing Models

My Notes

_____

_____

_____

_____

_____

Quick Lab continued

MODIFICATION FOR INDEPENDENT Inquiry

Explain to students that animals are adapted for the environments in which they live. Provide students with a materials list, and ask them to design a model that demonstrates how an animal with a lot of fur and insulation is better suited for life in an arctic biome than an animal with little or no fur is. After students have devised their plans and you have approved them, have students carry them out. Ask for volunteers to share their results with the class.

MODIFICATION FOR DIRECTED Inquiry

Provide students with the materials to complete the activity. Guide them as they fill each cup with hot water, place the lids on the cups, and insert thermometers in the holes in the lids. Have students label the cups A, B, and C. Explain that cup A represents an animal with no insulation, cup B represents an animal with a little insulation, and cup C represents an animal with a lot of insulation. Tell students to leave cup A as it is, but to add a layer of fabric to cup B and foam to cup C. Instruct students to record the temperature every 5 minutes (min) for 20 min. Provide a data chart for students to record their observations. At the end of 20 min, ask students to determine which cup retained the most heat. Based on their results, students should reason that the animal with the greatest amount of insulation is best suited for life in an arctic biome, whereas the animal without insulation is best suited for life in a warm biome.

Answer Key

1. Sample answer: I can leave one cup uncovered, cover another cup with wool cloth, and cover the third cup with foam rubber to represent the different levels of insulation.
   Teacher Prompt Why is a house insulated? (to keep in heat). An animal's body fat is a type of insulation, as is a mammal's fur.

4. Students' tables may vary, but should resemble the following:

Cup	Beginning temperature	5 Minutes	10 Minutes	15 Minutes	20 Minutes
A					
B					
C					

5. Cup A had the greatest decrease in temperature. Cup C had the least.

6. Cup B represents an animal best suited for a biome with moderate temperatures.

7. Sample answer: The tundra, because it would have more insulation for protection from the cold.

QUICK LAB GUIDED Inquiry

Which Biome?

In this activity, you will discover how animals are adapted for life in a particular biome. Some animals have little or no body fat or fur, whereas others have a great deal of both. Body fat and fur act as insulation to protect animals from extremely cold temperatures.

PROCEDURE

① Devise a plan to use the materials given to you by your teacher to create models of three different animals: an animal with little body fat and no fur, an animal with some body fat and some fur, and an animal with a lot of body fat and fur.

_____

_____

_____

_____

② Label the cups A, B, and C. Have cup A represent an animal with no insulation, cup B represent an animal with some insulation, and cup C represent an animal with a lot of insulation. Fill each cup with an equal amount of hot water. Fit the lid tightly on each cup and insert a thermometer in the hole in each lid. In the chart in Step 5, record the water temperature in each cup.

③ Carry out your plan from Step 1.

④ Make a chart to record the temperature in each cup. Check the temperature of each cup every 5 minutes (min) for a total of 20 min, and record each temperature in your chart.

OBJECTIVES

- Model how insulation helps animals regulate their body temperature in cold temperatures.
- Infer which animals are best suited for life in extremely cold biomes.

MATERIALS

For each pair
- cloth, wool
- cup, plastic with lid (3)
- foam (or other flexible insulating material)
- tape, masking
- thermometers (3)
- water, heated

For each student
- lab apron
- safety goggles

Quick Lab continued

5 Which cup had the greatest decrease in temperature? Which had the least?

_____

_____

6 Which cup represents an animal best suited for a biome with moderate temperatures, such as a temperate grassland? Explain.

_____

_____

_____

7 Which biome would the animal represented by cup C be best suited for: the tundra or a rain forest? Explain.

_____

_____

_____

FIELD LAB GUIDED *Inquiry* **AND** INDEPENDENT *Inquiry*

What's in an Ecosystem? GENERAL

👥 Small groups
🕐 Two 45-minute class periods

LAB RATINGS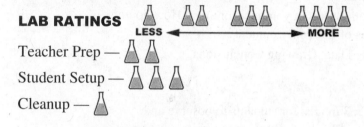

Teacher Prep —
Student Setup —
Cleanup —

MATERIALS

For each group
- field guides to local plants and animals
- hammer
- magnifying lens
- markers or colored pencils, several different colors
- meterstick or tape measure
- notebook
- pen or pencil
- poster board or construction paper
- small jars or paper cups
- stakes (at least 4)
- string (15 m)
- trowels, forks, and/or spoons

For each student
- lab apron
- safety goggles

SAFETY INFORMATION

On the day before the lab, tell students to wear appropriate clothing for this activity. Provide aprons for those who come to school dressed otherwise.

Remind students to review all safety cautions and icons before beginning this lab.

TEACHER NOTES

In this activity, students will observe a local ecosystem and make a study of the different biotic and abiotic factors in it. Before you have students perform this lab, obtain as many field guides about the natural history of your region as possible. Public and school libraries, as well as used bookstores, should have these guides. Internet research may also yield results. Encourage groups to study the field guides before they perform the lab so they do not go into the field unprepared. Make sure to have field guides available at the site for students to refer back to. Award points to groups that use the field guides to correctly identify plants and animals in their plots.

Assign two to three students per plot. Instruct students not to trespass on plots assigned to other groups. If the plots are contiguous, there should be a lane between rows of plots so students can access their plots without stepping on another plot.

Encourage groups to pick a terrain that has a variety of features to survey. If you have additional time for this activity, have groups switch plots until every group has surveyed every area. Save the results of this lab each year so that students in later years can compare their results and see how the ecosystem has changed over time.

Tell students to pick a spot that is fairly undisturbed. If your school is in an urban area, try surveying the school grounds or a nearby park. To make the lab go quicker, prepare the plot stakes by tying 3 meter (m) sections of string to the stakes before beginning the activity. Have students discuss their expectations ahead of the activity: what organisms live in the site, what abiotic factors can be found, and how the organisms interact with those abiotic factors. Encourage students to write their expectations in their notes and to review them at the end of the lab.

My Notes

_____

_____

_____

_____

_____

Field Lab continued

This field lab provides an excellent opportunity for long-term data collection. If possible, have students revisit their sites to gather data at least once during each season. At the end of the year, have them compile all the data into a report that shows how things in the ecosystem changed with the seasons.

Tip This activity helps students understand the living and nonliving parts of an ecosystem and how they interact, as well as the organization of things in an ecosystem.

Student Tip Think about how you interact with things in your environment. How do you think other organisms interact with the features of their environment?

Skills Focus Making Observations, Analyzing Data, Drawing Conclusions

MODIFICATION FOR DIRECTED Inquiry

Before beginning the activity, stake off a 3 m × 3 m area for students to observe and a smaller (1 m × 1 m) area within the larger area. Work with students to write a list of everything they need to observe: how many organisms they find and what kind, what those organisms feed on, what nonliving things are found in the area, and so on. Encourage students to use a camera to take pictures of the area. Pictures can be enlarged and annotated in lieu of a student-drawn map. Demonstrate how to annotate the pictures; for example, if there are five blue birds in a tree, draw five blue circles on the tree and add the symbol to a key. Have students work in groups. At the end of the activity, have each group present their findings.

Answer Key for GUIDED Inquiry

ASK A QUESTION

1. Answers will vary. Most students will expect to observe different organisms interacting with their ecosystem.
   Teacher Prompt Remember to think about how all living things in the ecosystem are affected, including insects and plants.

MAKE OBSERVATIONS

3. Sample answer: I will include all stationary objects, such as buildings, streams, rocks, trees and other plants, hills, and other land features. I will use symbols to record the type of organisms found and the number of each type.
   Teacher Prompt Show students different types of maps to help them choose a style for their map.

4. Check students' maps to make sure they accurately depict the area being surveyed.

5. Check students' notebooks to make sure their observations represent the area they are observing.

7. Sample answer: I can use a magnifying glass to examine the organism and its environment closely.

8. Check students' notebooks to make sure their observations are an accurate reflection of the organism they are studying.

Field Lab continued

ANALYZE THE RESULTS

9. Students' paragraphs will vary but should all contain similar descriptions of the larger area surveyed.

10. Students' descriptions may include a physical description of the animal and its niche in the ecosystem.

DRAW CONCLUSIONS

11. Students' answers should describe how sunlight, water, and other abiotic factors impact the organism chosen.

12. Answers will vary. Accept all reasonable answers.

Connect TO THE ESSENTIAL QUESTION

13. Sample answer: Abiotic factors can be important in limiting what organisms can live in a particular ecosystem. They can impact an ecosystem in a large way.

Answer Key for INDEPENDENT Inquiry

ASK A QUESTION

1. Answers will vary. Most students will expect to observe different organisms interacting with their ecosystem.
Teacher Prompt Remember to think about how all living things in the ecosystem are affected, including insects and plants.

DEVELOP A PLAN

2. Students' plans will vary. Accept all reasonable plans.

3. Answers will vary. Accept all reasonable answers.

4. Answers will vary. Accept all reasonable answers.

ANALYZE RESULTS

6. Answers will vary. Accept all reasonable answers.

7. Students' paragraphs will vary but should all contain similar descriptions of the larger area surveyed.

8. Students' descriptions may include a physical description of the animal and its niche in the ecosystem.

DRAW CONCLUSIONS

9. Students' answers should describe how sunlight, water, and other abiotic factors impact the organism chosen.

10. Answers will vary. Accept all reasonable answers.

Connect TO THE ESSENTIAL QUESTION

11. Sample answer: Abiotic factors can be important in limiting what organisms can live in a particular ecosystem. Abiotic factors can impact an ecosystem in a large way.

FIELD LAB GUIDED *Inquiry*

What's in an Ecosystem?

How well do you know the environment around your home or school? You may walk through it every day without noticing most of the living things it contains or without thinking about how they survive. In this lab, you will play the role of an ecologist by closely observing part of your environment. You will determine an organism's role in the ecosystem and will analyze the relationship between the organism and the abiotic and biotic factors in the ecosystem.

PROCEDURE

ASK A QUESTION

1 In this lab you will observe an ecosystem. What do you expect to observe during this activity?

_____

_____

_____

_____

MAKE OBSERVATIONS

2 Use a meterstick to measure a 3 meter (m) × 3 m area to study. Use the stakes to mark off the corners of the site. Tie the string to the stakes to create a boundary around your site. This is the area that you will observe.

3 How can you make a map to show all the features of the area as well as all the organisms living in the area?

_____

_____

_____

4 Make your map.

5 Observe the abiotic features in the area. List them in your notebook and describe how they affect the area.

OBJECTIVES

- Distinguish between abiotic and biotic features in an ecosystem.
- Identify an organism's habitat and niche.

MATERIALS

For each group
- field guides to local plants and animals
- hammer
- magnifying lens
- markers or colored pencils, several different colors
- meterstick or tape measure
- notebook
- pen or pencil
- poster board or construction paper
- small jars or paper cups
- stakes (at least 4)
- string (15 m)
- trowels, forks, and/or spoons

For each student
- lab apron
- safety goggles

Field Lab continued

6 When you have completed your observations of the area, identify a 1 m × 1 m section of the area that you would like to observe in greater detail. Stake out the area and set up a boundary.

7 How can you best examine the role of an organism in the smaller area? Write a plan.

_____

_____

_____

_____

8 Carry out your plan. Record your observations in your notebook.

ANALYZE THE RESULTS

9 **Describing Observations** Write a paragraph that describes the 3 m × 3 m area you observed.

_____

_____

_____

_____

10 **Analyzing Data** Describe the organism you observed and its role in the ecosystem.

_____

_____

_____

_____

DRAW CONCLUSIONS

11 **Evaluating Data** How is the organism you chose affected by the abiotic features in the ecosystem?

_____

_____

_____

_____

Field Lab continued

⑫ **Making Predictions** Choose one of the abiotic factors in the ecosystem. How would the ecosystem be different without that factor?

_____

_____

_____

_____

Connect **TO THE ESSENTIAL QUESTION**

⑬ **Describing Concepts** Why is it important to consider both living and nonliving things when discussing an ecosystem?

_____

_____

FIELD LAB INDEPENDENT *Inquiry*

What's in an Ecosystem?

How well do you know the environment around your home or school? You may walk through it every day without noticing most of the living things it contains or without thinking about how they survive. In this lab, you will play the role of an ecologist by closely observing part of your environment. You will determine an organism's role in the ecosystem, and you will analyze the relationship between the organism and the abiotic and biotic factors in its ecosystem.

PROCEDURE

ASK A QUESTION

❶ In this lab you will observe an ecosystem. What do you think you will observe during this activity?

_____

_____

_____

_____

DEVELOP A PLAN

❷ In the following space, describe an experimental setup and procedure that will allow you to observe an organism in its environment. Use the materials listed on the page. Remember: Do not disturb the ecosystem while making your observations.

_____

_____

_____

_____

OBJECTIVES

- Distinguish between abiotic and biotic features in an ecosystem.
- Identify an organism's habitat and niche.

MATERIALS

For each group
- field guides to local plants and animals
- hammer
- magnifying lens
- markers or colored pencils, several different colors
- meterstick or tape measure
- notebook
- pen or pencil
- poster board or construction paper
- small jars or paper cups
- stakes (at least 4)
- string (15 m)
- trowels, forks, and/or spoons

For each student
- lab apron
- safety goggles

Field Lab continued

❸ What data will you collect during your experiment? How will you share your data with the class?

_____

_____

_____

_____

❹ How can you use your observations to determine an organism's role in the ecosystem?

_____

_____

MAKE OBSERVATIONS

❺ Show your proposed procedure to your teacher. When your teacher approves your procedure, carry it out. Record your observations in your notebook. Use poster board to create any visual images used as part of your observations.

ANALYZE THE RESULTS

❻ **Evaluating Methods** Evaluate your experimental setup and procedure. Are there any modifications you would make to your setup?

_____

_____

_____

_____

❼ **Describing Observations** Write a paragraph that describes your observations.

_____

_____

_____

_____

Field Lab continued

8 **Analyzing Data** Choose one of the organisms you observed and describe its role in the ecosystem.

_____

_____

_____

_____

DRAW CONCLUSIONS

9 **Evaluating Data** How is the organism you chose affected by the abiotic factors in the ecosystem?

_____

_____

_____

_____

10 **Making Predictions** Choose one of the abiotic factors in the ecosystem. How would the ecosystem be different if that factor was absent?

_____

_____

_____

_____

Connect TO THE ESSENTIAL QUESTION

11 **Describing Concepts** Why is it important to consider the nonliving as well as the living things when discussing an ecosystem?

_____

_____

QUICK LAB GUIDED Inquiry

Making Compost GENERAL

👥 Small groups

🕐 20 minutes, plus additional observation time as scheduled by student groups

LAB RATINGS

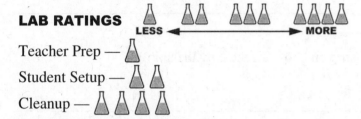

LESS ◄─────► MORE

Teacher Prep —

Student Setup —

Cleanup —

SAFETY INFORMATION

Remind students to review all safety cautions and icons before beginning this lab. Be certain that students wear gloves, goggles, and aprons when working with the compost. As the material decomposes, fungi and mold may spread, and students should not come in direct contact with these organisms. Students with allergies should avoid contact with compost. Avoid meat, dairy, and pet wastes as part of your compost materials. Avoid high sugar contents and strong odors to help control pests that might be attracted to the compost.

TEACHER NOTES

In this activity, students will design and fill a compost bin to observe decomposition of organic wastes. Compost bins will be subjected to a range of environmental factors to test how those variables affect decomposition.

Encourage each student group to discuss the observations they should make, the types of data they will be collecting, and how they will organize and display the data. Students should also consider how they will interpret their data to determine the best combinations of air, water, and light for decomposition to occur. In general, compost that is well ventilated, mixed often, kept consistently moist throughout, and exposed to daylight will decompose quicker and more thoroughly than otherwise. Direct sunlight increases the overall temperature of the compost and encourages organisms such as worms to burrow deep into the compost, which benefit decomposition.

For kitchen wastes, use vegetable peelings, fruit cores, coffee grounds, leftover meals, other non-meat/dairy organic wastes, etc. For yard wastes, use grass clippings, leaves, dead houseplants, sawdust, wood chips, and bark.

Tip This activity may help students better understand the factors that affect organic decomposition.

MATERIALS

For each group

- box with lid, at least 6 inches deep
- graduated cylinder, at least 125 mL
- kitchen waste (enough to make a layer 1–3 inches thick)
- plastic bag, sealable
- potting soil (enough to make a layer 1–3 inches thick)
- ruler
- scissors
- stirring stick
- straws
- water
- yard wastes (enough to make a layer 2–4 inches thick)

For each student
- gloves
- lab apron
- safety goggles

My Notes

_____

_____

_____

_____

_____

Quick Lab continued

Skills Focus Developing Procedures, Making Observations, Drawing Conclusions

MODIFICATION FOR DIRECTED Inquiry

Provide students with step-by-step instructions for designing and building their compost bins. Instruct them to cut holes in the lid of the box for ventilation. Direct them to add layers of organic material 3–5 cm thick. Tell them to add enough water to moisten the mixture and then stir it thoroughly. Have them place boxes on a windowsill and add water and stir every two days for two weeks. They should record their observations each time in a lab notebook, including how much water was added, how much light the boxes receive, and the progress of decomposition. At the end of the investigation, they should answer questions 5, 6, and 7 on the Student Worksheet.

MODIFICATION FOR INDEPENDENT Inquiry

Have students propose an experimental procedure to investigate the factors that affect decomposition. Students should create a procedure that describes an experiment to test the effect of a variable on decomposition rate, including all materials and the experimental setup. They should create data tables for recording data and observations and analyzing results. With teacher approval, they should carry out their experiments and present their conclusions in a lab report.

Answer Key

1. Accept all reasonable answers.

3. Accept all reasonable answers.

5. Sample answer: water

   Teacher Prompt Based on what you saw and the other students in the class shared, what seems to be important for allowing decomposing organisms to quickly break down organic waste? Sample answer: air, light, and water

6. Sample answer: We did not add very much water to our compost bin, and the wastes did not decompose very well.

7. Sample answer: Without decomposition, dead matter would be piled up all around us.

QUICK LAB GUIDED **Inquiry**

Making Compost

In this lab, you will design, build, and maintain a compost bin to investigate how air, water, and light affect the decomposition of organic materials. Many gardeners put unwanted yard waste into a pile to be broken down by decomposer organisms such as bacteria, protists, fungi, worms, and insects. This pile of decomposing matter is called *compost* and is a natural kind of fertilizer. Decomposers are an important part of the life cycle. When leaves fall from a tree, they accumulate on the ground. Without decomposers to help them break down, dead leaves and other dead organic matter would cover Earth. Decomposers break down organic waste, produce gases such as methane, and provide nutrients to the soil, water, and air.

PROCEDURE

❶ Examine your **box** and the tools and organic materials your teacher has provided. Decide how you will use the materials to create a compost bin. Decide how you will combine the **yard waste**, **kitchen waste**, and **potting soil** in the box. Will you add water? Will you ventilate the box? Will you allow light to penetrate the box? Create an experimental setup, and describe your design below.

_____

_____

_____

_____

_____

_____

_____

❷ When your teacher has approved your design, build your compost bin. Decide where you will store your compost bin for the duration of the experiment. Make sure to get teacher approval, and then place your box in the designated area.

OBJECTIVES

- Describe organic decomposition.
- Investigate how cellular respiration breaks down food to provide energy and releases carbon dioxide.

MATERIALS

For each group
- box with lid
- graduated cylinder, at least 125 mL
- kitchen waste
- plastic bag, sealable
- potting soil
- ruler
- scissors
- stirring stick
- straws
- water
- yard wastes

For each student
- gloves
- lab apron
- safety goggles

Quick Lab continued

3 Design a schedule to observe your compost box during the next two weeks. How often will you check the progress of decomposition? How often will you stir your compost? Will you add more water? How much? How much light will it receive? Decide what data you will record and how you will record them. Describe your procedure below.

_____

_____

_____

_____

_____

_____

4 When your teacher has approved your procedure, follow your schedule for the next two weeks and record your observations in your lab notebook. At the end of the experiment, answer the questions below.

5 What is needed for decomposition to occur?

_____

_____

6 How did the amounts of air, water, and light you allowed affect your compost pile?

_____

_____

_____

_____

7 Why is decomposition important?

_____

_____

_____

_____

_____

_____

QUICK LAB **DIRECTED** *Inquiry*

Energy Role Game GENERAL

👥 Small groups
🕐 20 minutes

MATERIALS
For the class
- descriptive clues (9)
- timer

LAB RATINGS

LESS ←————————→ MORE

Teacher Prep —
Student Setup —
Cleanup —

My Notes
_____
_____
_____
_____
_____

TEACHER NOTES

In this activity, you will read descriptions of a variety of organisms one at a time. For each description, write the scientific name on the board so students can see it. Students work in groups to discuss the clues given in the descriptions to decide what energy role the organism plays and also to guess the identity of the organism. Points are awarded to each team for correctly identifying each organism's energy role and for identifying each organism.

A set of nine descriptions is provided below. Feel free to add to this list yourself or have a student work on it as an independent project. A good source of information for scientific names and descriptions is the Encyclopedia of Life website, http://www.eol.org/. Mix up the order so that there is no pattern to the series of descriptions you read.

EXAMPLE DESCRIPTIONS:

1. My scientific name is *Theobroma cacao*. I live in tropical areas of South America. You may never have seen examples of my species, but if you have ever had hot cocoa or eaten a candy bar, you've eaten some of me. [answer: cacao (cocoa) plant, producer]

2. My scientific name is *Accipiter cooperii*. I live in North America ranging from Canada to Mexico. I don't eat bird seed and I prey on smaller animals, but sometimes I find my food at bird feeders in winter months. [answer: Cooper's hawk, consumer]

3. My scientific name is *Amanita phalloides*. I am a fungus that lives in dark, damp places in woodlands. I am very poisonous when eaten. I do a good job of breaking down fallen logs. [answer: death cap mushroom, decomposer]

4. My scientific name is *Pinus ponderosa*. I live in North America and have a long life span but stay in one spot my whole life. Some beetles like to eat me. [answer: ponderosa pine tree, producer]

5. My scientific name is *Apis mellifera*. I always seem to cause a buzz wherever I go. Many people find my stinger to be frightening. [answer: common honey bee, consumer]

6. My scientific name is *Musca domestica*. I start life as an egg, become a pupa, and finally become an adult. I am commonly considered a pest and I hang out around garbage and any food that smells whether it is good or bad. [answer: house fly, decomposer]

7. My scientific name is *Chlamydomonas reinhardtii*. I live in freshwater and like to stay near the surface. In fact, I float around all day and don't bother anyone. If enough of us get together, we can make a pretty big, green mat on the surface of the water. [answer: green algae, producer]

8. My scientific name is *Crotalus ruber*. I live in the hills of Southern California. I have diamond-shaped patterns on my back and cause quite the rattle if I am disturbed. I love the sun but have to hide in the shadows while I wait for a meal to come along. [red diamond rattlesnake, consumer]

9. My scientific name is *Dictyostelium mucoroides*. You can probably guess my energy role by hearing that my common name has the word "slime" in it. I like to live in damp, dark places and don't hurt anything. At some point in my life cycle, I produce a fruiting body to release spores. [slime mold, decomposer]

Tip This activity will help familiarize students with scientific names and start them thinking about how various organisms obtain energy from their environment.

Student Tip Use the clues to think about how the organism obtains energy from the environment. Sometimes, the scientific name can help you guess the common name of the organism. You don't necessarily have to be able to identify the organism; you just have to be able to think about how it obtains its energy.

Skills Focus Classifying Organisms, Applying Concepts

MODIFICATION FOR GUIDED Inquiry

Have students research their own clues to use in this game.

Answer Key

3. See correct answers in Teacher Notes.
4. Accept all reasonable answers.
5. Accept all reasonable answers.
6. Accept all reasonable answers.

QUICK LAB DIRECTED *Inquiry*

Energy Role Game

All organisms require a source of energy to live. We can classify organisms into three major groups according to the source of energy they use. Producers are organisms that convert radiant energy from the sun to make food for themselves. Consumers are organisms that eat other organisms as their source of energy. Decomposers are a type of consumer that obtains their energy by breaking down the remains of other organisms.

In this activity, you will work in small groups to play a game in which you work to identify the energy roles and the identities of different organisms. Use the clues provided for each organism to think about the way that organisms takes in energy from the environment. Even if you can't guess the identity of the organism, the clues may help you identify its energy role.

OBJECTIVES

- Draw conclusions about the energy role of each organism described.
- Use clues to guess the identity of each organism.

MATERIALS

For the class
- descriptive clues (9)
- timer

PROCEDURE

1 Form small groups of three or four. Sit together so that you can easily talk softly among yourselves to discuss the clues.

2 Your teacher will write the scientific name of an organism on the board and then read the description of that organism and start a timer immediately following the reading. You will have one minute total for each organism. First, write down the the common name of the organism and its energy role (producer, consumer, or decomposer). After writing down your guess, talk softly with your group and share information with each other. Then decide the common name and energy role for the organism and write it in the appropriate place on the table. When the minute is up, your teacher will move on to the next organism.

Quick Lab continued

❸ Record your answers below.

Organism	Identity		Energy role	
	My answer	Group answer	My answer	Group answer
1				
2				
3				
4				
5				
6				
7				
8				
9				

❹ At the end of the timed session, your teacher will reveal the identities of the organisms. Give your group one point for every energy role guessed correctly. Give your group one point for every organism you were able to identify in a general way. Give your group an extra bonus point for every organism you were able to identify specifically. Count up your points to see how well you did.

_____

❺ Were there any organisms that you could not identify by name but you could identify in terms of the energy role they play? Why were you able to identify that organism's energy role?

_____

_____

_____

❻ Were there any organisms that you could identify by name but you did not correctly identify their energy role? Why do you think you were mistaken about that organism's energy role?

_____

_____

_____

Food Webs GENERAL

👥 Small groups

🕐 One 20-minute class period plus two 45-minute class periods

LAB RATINGS

LESS ⬅————➡ MORE

Teacher Prep —

Student Setup —

Cleanup —

MATERIALS

For each group
- binoculars
- camera
- field notebook
- local field guides (plants, animals)
- magnifying lens
- markers, colored
- pencil (or pen)
- poster board

For each student
- protective clothing
- protective gloves

SAFETY INFORMATION

Remind students to review all safety cautions and icons before beginning this lab. Caution students to use care when moving about natural areas that may be uneven or slippery. Be sure students know which plants and animals are harmful and also know to avoid any of these organisms and alert you to their presence. Attempt to learn about any allergies or sensitivities to plants or insect stings or bites that any students might have.

TEACHER NOTES

In this activity, students will work in small groups to conduct field research in a local natural area to identify local food webs. If a suitable natural area is not convenient to the school, make arrangements to take students to a nearby city aquarium, botanical garden, or park for their field investigation. Back in the classroom, groups will diagram the transfer of energy in the food webs identified during their field research, making inferences based on their observations. It is best to conduct this activity after students have a solid understanding of the energy pyramid and food webs and can explain the relationships among producers, consumers (primary, secondary, and tertiary), and decomposers. You may want to review these concepts just before students begin this activity.

For the Guided Inquiry option, allow students a 20-minute period before the field investigation to plan their work. Then allow one full class period for the field study and a second full class period for analysis.

Tip This activity will help students learn how to conduct a field investigation.

Student Tip During your field investigation, be sure to look carefully so that you do not overlook small organisms or ones that are well-camouflaged.

Skills Focus Making Observations, Making Inferences, Describing Relationships

My Notes

_____

_____

_____

_____

_____

Field Lab continued

MODIFICATION FOR DIRECTED Inquiry

Instead of having students work in small groups, have the class work as one group. Begin the activity as described for the Guided Inquiry version. Following the field study, have all students work together to review the information and apply it to construct one food web model for the entire class.

Answer Key for GUIDED Inquiry

MAKE OBSERVATIONS

3. Accept all reasonable answers. Be sure that students observe some of each type of organism: producer, consumer, and decomposer.

BUILD A MODEL

4. Accept all reasonable answers.
5. Accept all reasonable answers.
6. Accept all reasonable answers.

ANALYZE THE RESULTS

7. Answers will vary. Students should recognize that in some cases, they did not directly observe energy relationships between the organisms they studied. This caused them to have to make inferences that may have led to the introduction of some inaccuracies in their food web model. They should suggest more field study to collect more accurate data and/or observations about energy relationships between the organisms.
8. Accept all reasonable answers.

Connect TO THE ESSENTIAL QUESTION

9. Accept all reasonable answers. Students should explain the flow of energy from the sun to producers to consumers and/or decomposers, naming the organisms they studied as examples to back up their explanation.

Answer Key for INDEPENDENT Inquiry

DEVELOP A PLAN

2. Accept all reasonable answers. Be sure that the plan includes a table for recording observations.

MAKE OBSERVATIONS

4. Accept all reasonable answers. Be sure that students observe some of each type of organism: producer, consumer, and decomposer.

BUILD A MODEL

5. Accept all reasonable answers.
7. Accept all reasonable answers.

Field Lab continued

ANALYZE THE RESULTS

8. Accept all reasonable answers. Students should recognize that in some cases, they did not directly observe energy relationships between the organisms they studied. This caused them to have to make inferences, which may have led to the introduction of some inaccuracies in their food web model. They should suggest more field study to collect more accurate data and/or observations about energy relationships between the organisms.

9. Accept all reasonable answers.

Connect TO THE ESSENTIAL QUESTION

10. Accept all reasonable answers. Students should explain the flow of energy from the sun to producers to consumers and/or decomposers, naming the organisms they studied as examples to back up their explanation.

Food Webs

In this lab, you will do field research in a local natural area to observe the organisms living in your area. From your observations, you will make inferences about the energy relationships between these organisms and use the information to construct a food web diagram.

Living things are connected to other living things by their energy needs. Plants obtain their energy from the sun and convert this energy into a form that other organisms can use. Plants are therefore considered to be producers. Producers supply energy for many organisms, including all animals and many bacteria, fungi, and protists, either directly or indirectly.

Many animals and some bacteria, fungi, and protists consume plants, other organisms, or both. Because they obtain their energy through the food they eat, these organisms are considered to be consumers. Some animals and many bacteria, fungi, and protists act as decomposers, which consume the remains of other organisms. Decomposers are a type of consumer.

PROCEDURE

ASK A QUESTION

1 In this lab, you will investigate the following question: What are the relationships among producers, consumers, and decomposers in a local natural area?

MAKE OBSERVATIONS

2 Travel to the natural area you will be studying. Do not touch or approach animals and use care to avoid touching plants unless you know them to be safe to touch. Consult your teacher if you have any doubts about handling any plants.

OBJECTIVES

- Observe the living organisms in a local natural area.
- Use observations to infer relationships among producers, consumers, and decomposers in the natural area.

MATERIALS

For each group
- binoculars
- camera
- field notebook
- local field guides (plants, animals)
- magnifying lens
- markers, colored
- pencil (or pen)
- poster board

For each student
- protective clothing
- protective gloves

Field Lab continued

3 Examine and describe all organisms that you observe. As you work, refer to any field guides provided by your teacher to learn about the organisms you see. Record their names and a description of each in the table below. Include any observations of eating behavior. Sketch illustrations of each organism and write a short note about each sketch in your notebook. If you use a camera instead of sketching the organism, make a note of it in your notebook for later reference. If you found only one, more than one, or a large group of the same organism, write that in your notebook. Be sure that you make observations of all three types of organisms: producers, consumers, and decomposers.

FIELD OBSERVATIONS OF ORGANISMS

Name of organism	Description of physical appearance, location, and behavior	Role in the ecosystem (producer, consumer, decomposer)

Field Lab continued

BUILD A MODEL

4 Back in the classroom, work with your group to discuss the energy relationships among the organisms you observed. Using a blank sheet of paper, sketch a food web model for these organisms as your group discusses the relationships. Label each organism as a producer, consumer, and/or decomposer. Some organisms may have more than one label. When you have a final sketch for a food web model that everyone agrees on, have your teacher approve it.

5 Make a larger version of your food web model on a piece of poster board using colored markers. Include sketches or photos of the organisms from your field notes.

6 Present your model to the other groups in the class. Explain each organism you observed, its energy role, and how it is connected to all of the other organisms in the food web.

ANALYZE THE RESULTS

7 **Analyzing Observations** As you created your model, how often did you find that you had to make inferences about the energy relationships among the organisms you observed? Do you think all of these inferences resulted in accurate information shown in your model? What could you do to improve the accuracy of the information shown in your food web?

_____

_____

_____

_____

_____

8 **Evaluating Results** Were there any sections of the food web that you found to be incomplete? Describe an example of one of these areas and explain why you felt this way.

_____

_____

_____

_____

_____

Field Lab continued

Connect TO THE ESSENTIAL QUESTION

9 **Identifying Patterns** Use the food web model you created from this investigation to explain how energy flows through an ecosystem.

_____

_____

_____

_____

_____

FIELD LAB INDEPENDENT *Inquiry*

Food Webs

In this lab, you will do field research in a local natural area to observe the organisms living in your area. From your observations, you will make inferences about the energy relationships between these organisms and use the information to construct a food web diagram.

   Living things are connected to other living things by their energy needs. Plants obtain their energy from the sun and convert this energy into a form that other organisms can use. Plants are therefore considered to be producers. Producers supply energy for many organisms, including all animals and many bacteria, fungi, and protists, either directly or indirectly.

   Many animals and some bacteria, fungi, and protists consume plants, other organisms, or both. Because they obtain their energy through the food they eat, these organisms are considered to be consumers. Some animals and many bacteria, fungi, and protists act as decomposers, which consume the remains of other organisms. Decomposers are a type of consumer.

PROCEDURE

ASK A QUESTION

1 In this lab, you will investigate the following question: What are the relationships among producers, consumers, and decomposers in a local natural area?

OBJECTIVES

- Observe the living organisms in a local natural area.
- Use observations to infer relationships among producers, consumers, and decomposers in the natural area.

MATERIALS

For each group
- binoculars
- camera
- field notebook
- local field guides (plants, animals)
- magnifying lens
- markers, colored
- pencil (or pen)
- poster board

For each student
- protective clothing
- protective gloves

Field Lab continued

DEVELOP A PLAN

2 Work within your group to make a plan for answering the question in Step 1.
You will be able to travel to a natural area to carry out your plan. When everyone
in the group agrees on the plan, summarize it below. Your plan must include the
methods you will use in the field and how your group will record observations.
Obtain your teacher's approval when your group is finished with the plan.

_____

_____

_____

_____

_____

_____

_____

MAKE OBSERVATIONS

3 Travel to the natural area you will be studying. Do not touch or approach
animals, and use care to avoid touching plants unless you know them to be
safe to touch. Consult your teacher if you have any doubts about handling
any plants.

4 Carry out your plan for studying the natural area in a way that will allow
you to answer the question from Step 1.

BUILD A MODEL

5 Back in the classroom, work with your group to create a model to answer
the question from Step 1. When you have a final sketch for a model that
everyone agrees on have your teacher approve it.

6 Make a larger version of your model on a piece of poster board using
colored markers. Include sketches or photos of the organisms from your
field notes.

7 Present your model to the other groups in the class. Explain each part of
your model.

Field Lab continued

ANALYZE THE RESULTS

8 **Analyzing Observations** As you created your model, how often did you find that you had to make inferences about the energy relationships among the organisms you observed? Do you think all of these inferences resulted in accurate information shown in your model? What could you do to improve the accuracy of the information shown in your model?

_____

_____

_____

_____

_____

9 **Evaluating Results** Were there any sections of the model that you found to be incomplete? Describe an example of one of these areas and explain why you felt this way.

_____

_____

_____

_____

Connect TO THE ESSENTIAL QUESTION

10 **Identifying Patterns** Use the model you created from this investigation to explain how energy flows through an ecosystem.

_____

_____

_____

_____

_____

QUICK LAB DIRECTED Inquiry

What Factors Influence a Population Change? GENERAL

Student pairs

20 minutes

LAB RATINGS

LESS ◄────────► MORE

Teacher Prep —

Student Setup —

Cleanup —

Remind students to review all safety cautions and icons before beginning this lab. Ask students to be sure to pick up any popcorn kernels or dice that fall on the floor to avoid someone slipping on them.

TEACHER NOTES

In this activity, students model changes in the population size of a wolf pack that result from random natural events. Students use their results to make predictions.

Tip Be sure dice show only numbers 1 through 6. Make enough photocopies of the game key for each group to have two copies. Provide students with reading materials that describe and discuss different types of wolves.

Skills Focus Using Modeling, Making Inferences, Making Predictions

MODIFICATION FOR GUIDED Inquiry

Do not provide students with the game key included on the next page, but allow them to create their own game key before playing. This will cause students to think about how to effectively model changes that lead to population increases and decreases.

MATERIALS

For each pair
- cup
- dice (2)
- pencil
- popcorn kernels (generous handful)

My Notes

_____

_____

_____

_____

_____

Quick Lab continued

Answer Key

7. Answers will vary. Sample answer: Yes, my pack size was cut in half twice. After that, too many pups died.

8. Sample answer: Several events, such as food shortage and disease, occurring one after the other, cut the pack size quickly.

9. Sample answer: Species hunted by wolves might quickly grow in numbers and wipe out other parts of the food chain. As a result, many more animal and plant species could be affected.

Teacher Prompt What might happen to the rabbit population in the area where the wolves lived?

10. Sample answer: No. There are so many factors that affect a population; one must study a species in its environment to develop an more accurate model.

Teacher Prompt Did the game key cover all the possible factors that might affect a wolf population?

GAME KEY

If you roll. . .	You . . .	Reason
Double 2s, 3s, 4s, or 5s	Subtract 3	High pup mortality rate; three pups die (A)
2	Divide by 2 (round down)	Disease kills half the pack (B)
3	Follow Step 6	Food shortage occurs (C)
4 (1 + 3)	Subtract 1	One wolf dies of natural causes (D)
5	Subtract 1	Wolf killed in attack by another wolf pack (E)
6 (2 + 4 or 1 + 5)	Make no changes	Pack lives well for six months (F)
7	Make no changes	Pack lives well for six months (F)
8 (2 + 6 or 3 + 5)	Subtract 1	One pup dies (G)
9	Make no changes	Pack lives well for six months (F)
10 (4 + 6)	Subtract 1	Wolf killed in attack by another wolf pack (E)
11	Make no changes	Pack lives well for six months (F)
12	Add 1	New wolf joins pack (H)

QUICK LAB DIRECTED *Inquiry*

What Factors Influence
a Population Change?

During this lab, you will use popcorn kernels to simulate a pack of wolves. You will roll dice and use the numbers from the dice to represent changes that affect the wolf pack's survival.

PROCEDURE

1 Place eight popcorn kernels on the table. Two kernels represent adult wolves, and the other six represent a litter of pups.

2 Roll the dice to represent the passage of six months. Count the numbers on the dice and use that number to determine what happens to your pack according to the game key. Then fill in the appropriate information in your data table, as shown here. As you record data, refer to the Reason column in the game key, and write down the letter that refers to the number thrown on the dice. Adjust the number of kernels that represent your wolf pack.

OBJECTIVE
- Model factors that can increase or decrease the population size of a wolf pack.

MATERIALS

For each pair
- cup
- dice (2)
- pencil
- popcorn kernels (generous handful)

DATA TABLE

Year	Last year's total	Add a litter (+6)	First 6 months Reason	First 6 months Effect on pack	Second 6 months Reason	Second 6 months Effect on pack	Pack subtotal	Subtract matured pups?	Total pack for year
1	2	+6						No	
2								No	
3									
4									
5									
6									
7									
8									
9									
10									
11									
12									
13									
14									
15									

Quick Lab continued

3 Repeat Step 2 for the second six months. Count the number of wolves in your pack and fill in the rest of Year 1 in the data table.

4 Reproduction: After Year 1, add six pups at the beginning of each year unless a food shortage occurred the previous year. Adjust the number of kernels accordingly.

5 Maturation: When the pack gets too large, the mature pups leave. Subtract six wolves if your pack has more than nine wolves. Adjust the number of kernels accordingly and record the pack total in the last column of the table.

6 Repeat Steps 2–5 until you complete 15 years of play or until your pack dies out, whichever occurs first.

7 Did your team's pack die out during the game? How?

_____

_____

8 What reasons led to the fastest loss of a pack?

_____

_____

9 How could the disappearance of wolves from an ecosystem affect the populations of other species?

_____

_____

_____

10 Do you feel this game accurately modeled the changing population of a wolf pack? Explain your answer.

_____

_____

_____

QUICK LAB INDEPENDENT Inquiry

Investigate an Abiotic Limiting Factor GENERAL

MATERIALS

For each group
• cups, paper (2)
• pencil
• ruler, metric
• seeds, bean (20–30)
• soil, potting (1 cup)
• water

For each student
• lab apron
• safety goggles

Small groups

30 minutes

LAB RATINGS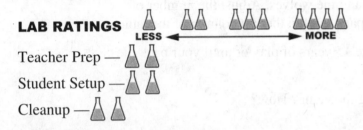

Teacher Prep —

Student Setup —

Cleanup —

SAFETY INFORMATION

Remind students to review all safety cautions and icons before beginning this lab. Ask students to clean up any soil that spills and discard it in the proper waste container. Have students wash and dry their hands at the completion of this activity.

My Notes

_____

_____

_____

_____

_____

TEACHER NOTES

In this activity, students will choose an abiotic factor that affects plant growth and will plan an investigation of that factor using the materials provided. Set up areas in the classroom where students may expose their plants to differences in common abiotic factors, such as amount of light, heat, or moisture.

Tip This activity will help students identify abiotic factors and teach them how to plan investigations.

Student Tip Consider all the things that plants need to grow, such as amount of living space.

Skills Focus Planning Investigations, Devising Procedures, Drawing Conclusions

MODIFICATION FOR GUIDED Inquiry

Provide students with the abiotic factor they are to investigate rather than asking them to choose this on their own. Also provide students with more background concerning the variable they will use in setting up their experiments. For example, if you ask students to investigate the effect of varying light levels on plant growth, define what those light levels will be and what general method will be used achieve those lighting conditions.

Answer Key

2. Sample answers: amount of light, amount of living space, amount of water, room temperature.

3. Answers will vary.

   Teacher Prompt What will be different between the two cups? What factors will you change?

4. Sample answer: If bean seedlings get more light, then they will grow taller and become greener in color.

5. Answers will vary.

   Teacher Prompt How will you distribute the bean seeds between the two cups? Where will you put the cups after they are planted?

8. Answers will vary.

9. Sample answer: Yes. The bean seedlings grown under a light were greener in color than the seedlings that grew in the dark.

10. Answers will vary.

11. Accept all reasonable answers.

12. Accept all reasonable answers.

QUICK LAB INDEPENDENT *Inquiry*

Investigate an Abiotic Limiting Factor

In this lab, you will plan and conduct an investigation of how an abiotic factor affects the growth of bean seeds. Factors that affect the population size and health of living things are called *limiting factors*.

PROCEDURE

❶ Fill two 8-ounce (oz) paper cups with potting soil to within 1 centimeter (cm) of the top of each cup. Gently tap the cups on the lab table to settle the soil.

❷ Identify an abiotic factor present in the classroom that could affect the growth of plants.

Abiotic factor to investigate: _____

❸ Using only the materials listed, plan an experiment to test how the factor you chose affects the growth of plants. What will the variables be in your experiment?

_____

_____

❹ Write a hypothesis for your experiment.

_____

_____

❺ Describe the steps of the procedure. Include safety rules.

_____

_____

_____

_____

_____

OBJECTIVES

- Recognize abiotic factors in the environment.
- Design and conduct an investigation of the effect of an abiotic factor on bean seedlings.

MATERIALS

For each group
- cups, paper (2)
- pencil
- ruler, metric
- seeds, bean (20–30)
- soil, potting (1 cup)
- water

For each student
- lab apron
- safety goggles

Quick Lab continued

6 Get your teacher's approval to set up your experiment. Teacher's initials:

_____

7 Set up your experiment. Check the cups periodically and collect data after two weeks.

8 Make a data table in the space below and record your results in it.

9 Were there any differences between the plants in each cup? Explain.

_____

_____

10 Was your hypothesis supported or not supported by your data? Explain.

_____

_____

11 Write the conclusion for your experiment.

_____

_____

12 How might you have improved your procedure to obtain clearer results?

_____

_____

_____

EXPLORATION LAB DIRECTED Inquiry AND GUIDED Inquiry

How Do Populations Interact? GENERAL

👥 Small groups

🕐 45 minutes

LAB RATINGS

LESS ←——————→ MORE

Teacher Prep —

Student Setup —

Cleanup —

MATERIALS

For each group

- black beans, dry (generous handful)
- colored pencils (3)
- pencil
- penny
- red beans, dry (generous handful)
- ruler
- white beans, dry (generous handful)

TEACHER NOTES

In this activity, students will explore how the populations in a community affect one another. You may want to assign individual group members to be responsible for each population.

The materials listed are enough for a group of three students. You may want to prepare bags of premeasured beans ahead of time to simplify the distribution of materials. Any differently colored items that are like-sized, such as buttons, beads, or coins, can replace the dried beans. The colored pencils are intended for use in the graphing section but can be replaced by markers or regular pencils.

Draw an example graph so that students can see how to set the graph up and plot the data points as they progress through the activity. Monitor student work in Step 6 to ensure that groups are making two sets of changes for each phase—the prescribed seasonal changes as well as the appropriate scenario changes.

While the simulation uses examples of biotic components, encourage students to think about how the scenarios directly affect abiotic factors, such as soil nutrients and water availability.

Skills Focus Creating Models, Making Graphs

MODIFICATION FOR INDEPENDENT Inquiry

Abiotic factors such as soil nutrients and water availability can also affect populations and population interactions. Have students develop a procedure to investigate how abiotic factors can affect populations and communities. They should develop a procedure that defines the materials they will use in their simulation and the data they will collect. With teacher approval, they should carry out their procedures and present their results and conclusions in a lab report.

My Notes

_____

_____

_____

_____

_____

Exploration Lab continued

Answer Key for DIRECTED Inquiry

MAKE A HYPOTHESIS

2. Accept all reasonable answers.

MAKE OBSERVATIONS

6. Accept all reasonable answers, but graphs should reflect the correct season and population counts.

7. Accept all reasonable answers, but students should show population numbers on the *y*-axis and seasons on the *x*-axis.
Teacher Prompt Remind students how to construct a line graph; if they need help, create a sample line graph on the board.

ANALYZE THE RESULTS

9. Answers will vary.

10. Sample answer: An increase in one population caused an increase in other populations because more food was available. But if a population increased too much, it used up all its resources and then the population decreased, as did the populations that depended on it.

11. Sample answer: Our population sizes are different from other groups' because different changes in the communities affected populations in different ways.

DRAW CONCLUSIONS

12. Sample answer: Because there is less sunlight in the winter, the clover population will probably shrink. This will affect the rabbit population because less food will be available. Also, the rabbits may no longer be breeding. These changes in the rabbit population will mean less food available for coyotes. So, all three populations will probably decline.

13. Sample answer: Results could be similar in a natural ecosystem. For example, changes like weather, disease, and breeding are all parts of a natural ecosystem. One important difference is that there would be many other populations involved in the community. This could play a role in determining population sizes.

Connect TO THE ESSENTIAL QUESTION

14. Sample answer: Changes in one population affect other populations because organisms rely on one another for food and other resources. Changes in populations could affect the environment because organisms must use abiotic resources, such as water, in order to survive and reproduce.

Exploration Lab continued

Answer Key for GUIDED Inquiry

MAKE A HYPOTHESIS

2. Accept all reasonable answers.

MAKE OBSERVATIONS

3. Sample answer: Different-colored beans can be used to represent different populations of organisms, such as grass, mice, and hawks.

4. Sample answer: I can change populations by adding or subtracting beans. If I add or subtract beans from one population, I have to add or subtract beans from the other populations depending on the relationships between them (producers, consumers, etc.).

5. Sample answer: I can record my data in a table and then analyze my data in a graph.

6. Accept all reasonable answers.

7. Accept all reasonable answers.

ANALYZE THE RESULTS

8. Answers will vary.

9. Sample answer: An increase in one population caused an increase in other populations because more food was available. But if a population increased too much, it used up all its resources and then the population decreased, as did the populations that depended on it.

DRAW CONCLUSIONS

10. Sample answer: Results could be similar in a natural ecosystem. For example, changes like weather, disease, and breeding are all parts of a natural ecosystem. One important difference is that there would be many other populations involved in the community. This could play a role in determining population sizes.

Connect TO THE ESSENTIAL QUESTION

11. Sample answer: Changes in one population affect other populations because organisms rely on one another for food and other resources. Changes in populations could affect the environment because organisms must use abiotic resources, such as water, in order to survive and reproduce.

EXPLORATION LAB DIRECTED Inquiry

How Do Populations Interact?

In this lab, you will simulate the interactions of populations in a community and observe how changes in populations affect one another and the environment. Communities are made of different populations interacting with one another. How do these interactions affect populations and the ecosystem in which they live? You will investigate various limiting factors in a mock ecosystem and their impact on native populations.

PROCEDURE

ASK A QUESTION

1 In this lab, you will investigate the following question: How do changes in populations affect communities?

MAKE A HYPOTHESIS

2 Think about the question, and form a hypothesis about the answer. Record your hypothesis below.

_____

_____

_____

_____

_____

OBJECTIVES

- Model the interactions of populations in an imaginary ecosystem.
- Describe how populations affect one another and their environment.

MATERIALS

For each group
- black beans, dry (generous handful)
- colored pencils (3)
- pencil
- penny
- red beans, dry (generous handful)
- ruler
- white beans, dry (generous handful)

MAKE OBSERVATIONS

3 Get **black**, **red**, and **white beans**; a **penny**; and three **colored pencils** from your teacher.

4 Sort the beans into like-colored piles. The white beans will represent the clover population, the black beans will represent the rabbit population, and the red beans will represent the coyote population.

Exploration Lab continued

5 Begin the simulation of a community in balance. Place twenty clover plants, twelve rabbits, and six coyotes in the center of your table. This represents the community at the beginning of spring.

6 User your **pencil** and **ruler** to create a line graph to illustrate population sizes. Use a different colored pencil to record data for each population. Draw your graph and plot the data for the beginning of spring in the space below.

7 Use the table below to model population sizes over three seasons, and record the data on your line graph. Follow these guidelines:

- Add or subtract beans for all of the population changes that occur in each activity. Organisms that do not eat enough food die. If a population reaches zero organisms at any time, there will not be any more of that organism for the remainder of the activity.

- For each season, make the seasonal changes first. Then, flip a **penny** to determine which scenario you will follow (heads or tails) to complete the season.

- After making changes to your model populations (by adding or subtracting beans), plot your population data on your graph above.

Exploration Lab continued

Season	Seasonal Changes	Heads Scenario	Tails Scenario
Spring	The clover population doubles. Each rabbit eats two clover plants in order to survive. Each coyote must eat one rabbit in order to survive.	Heavy spring rains allow fifteen additional new clover to grow. For every two rabbits, five new rabbits are born. Two coyotes die of disease.	For every two rabbits, six new rabbits are born. Construction in a nearby ecosystem drives three new coyotes to join the population.
Spring	The clover population triples. Each rabbit must eat two clover plants in order to survive. Each coyote must eat one rabbit in order to survive.	A late-summer drought kills half the clover population. For every two rabbits, two new rabbits are born. One coyote dies of dehydration.	Late-summer rains allow ten new clover plants to grow. For every two rabbits, six new rabbits are born.
Fall	The clover population doubles. Each rabbit must eat two clover plants in order to survive. Each coyote must eat one rabbit in order to survive.	Too many organisms are feeding on the clover, so half the clover population dies. Rabbits have trouble finding food, so five individuals die. Coyotes have trouble finding food, so two individuals die.	A warm fall means the clover population increases by nine plants. The weather and the abundance of food allow for a long breeding season. For every two rabbits, four new rabbits are born.

8 Draw lines on your graph to show the changes in population size for each organism. Use the same colored pencil for a single population for all seasons.

ANALYZE THE RESULTS

9 **Describing Results** Which populations were the most strongly affected by changes?

_____

_____

_____

_____

10 **Analyzing Results** How did changes to one population affect changes to the other populations?

_____

_____

_____

_____

_____

_____

Exploration Lab continued

⑪ Comparing Results Compare your group's results with those of another group. Are your final population sizes the same? Why or why not?

_____

_____

_____

_____

DRAW CONCLUSIONS

⑫ Interpreting Patterns How might winter affect the three populations in this activity?

_____

_____

_____

_____

⑬ Making Predictions Would you expect the same results in a natural ecosystem? Why or why not?

_____

_____

_____

_____

Connect TO THE ESSENTIAL QUESTION

⑭ Drawing Conclusions How do changes in one population affect other populations and the environment?

_____

_____

_____

_____

EXPLORATION LAB GUIDED *Inquiry*

How Do Populations Interact?

In this lab, you will simulate the interactions of populations in a community and observe how changes in populations affect one another and the environment. Communities are made of different populations interacting with one another. How do these interactions affect populations and the ecosystem in which they live? You will investigate various limiting factors in a mock ecosystem and their impact on native populations.

PROCEDURE

ASK A QUESTION

❶ In this lab, you will investigate the following question: How do changes in populations affect communities?

MAKE A HYPOTHESIS

❷ Think about the question, and form a hypothesis about the answer. Record your hypothesis below.

_____

_____

_____

_____

MAKE OBSERVATIONS

❸ Populations within a community are affected by the interactions between them. The growth or decline of one population may have a direct effect on another population within the community. In this activity, you will investigate how changes in populations affect one another. Design a procedure using the materials your teacher has provided to test the effects of population interactions. How can you use the materials to represent different populations?

_____

_____

_____

_____

_____

OBJECTIVES

- Model the interactions of populations in an imaginary ecosystem.
- Describe how populations affect one another and their environment.

MATERIALS

For each group
- black beans, dry (generous handful)
- colored pencils (3)
- pencil
- penny
- red beans, dry (generous handful)
- ruler
- white beans, dry (generous handful)

Exploration Lab continued

4 How can you change populations to observe how they affect one another?

_____

_____

_____

_____

5 How will you record data about population changes? How will you analyze your data?

_____

_____

_____

_____

_____

6 In the space below, describe your procedure to investigate the interactions between populations.

_____

_____

_____

_____

7 With teacher approval, carry out your experiment and record your results below.

_____

_____

_____

_____

ANALYZE THE RESULTS

8 **Describing Results** Which populations were the most strongly affected by changes?

_____

_____

_____

_____

Exploration Lab continued

⑨ Analyzing Results How did changes to one population affect changes to the other populations?

_____

_____

_____

_____

_____

DRAW CONCLUSIONS

⑩ Making Predictions Would you expect the same results in a natural ecosystem? Why or why not?

_____

_____

_____

_____

Connect TO THE ESSENTIAL QUESTION

⑪ Drawing Conclusions How do changes in one population affect other populations and the environment?

_____

_____

_____

_____

QUICK LAB GUIDED Inquiry

Prey Coloration GENERAL

Student pairs

30 minutes

LAB RATINGS

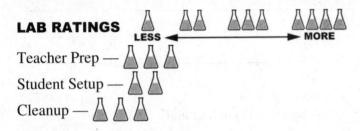

LESS ⟵⟶ MORE

Teacher Prep —

Student Setup —

Cleanup —

MATERIALS

For each pair
- cups to hold paper circles (3)
- paper, black, 8.5×11
- paper, newsprint, 8.5×11
- paper, white, 8.5×11
- paper circles, black
- paper circles, newsprint
- paper circles, white
- stopwatch

SAFETY INFORMATION

Remind students to review all safety cautions and icons before beginning this lab. If pieces of paper are laid on the floor, remind students that this poses a tripping hazard and to use care in stepping around the paper.

TEACHER NOTES

This activity models the effectiveness of camouflage in helping prey animals avoid being caught by predators. In the model, paper circles of black, white, or newsprint made using a hole-punch represent the prey. The students represent the predators. One student scatters 45 circles (15 of each kind) onto one black, one white, and one newsprint piece of paper. The stopwatch is started and a second student tries to capture as many circles as they can, grabbing one at a time within a one-minute time period. Students will find that they capture more circles on background paper of a different color, and fewer circles on background paper of the same color.

Tip Use a hole punch to prepare the paper circles and count them out prior to the lab to save time. Use small cups to hold 45 circles each, 15 of each color. There should be three cups per group, as each group will have three different colors of paper.

Skills Focus Developing Procedures, Making Tables, Drawing Conclusions

My Notes

_____

_____

_____

_____

_____

MODIFICATION FOR INDEPENDENT Inquiry

Provide students with the question, Does prey coloration affect an animal's ability to evade predators? Then have students develop their own experimental method, run their tests, and evaluate the results to answer the question.

Answer Key

2. Sample answer: We can compare how many prey circles the predator finds on each different color paper. We could use the stopwatch to make sure we use the same amount of time for each hunt.

3. Sample answer: More prey animals survive when their coloring is similar to the coloring of their environment because predators will have a harder time seeing them.

4. Sample answer: More prey animals survive when their coloring is the coloring of their environment because predators cannot easily see them.

5. Sample data table:

		Number of prey captured in one minute		
		Black	Printed	White
Type of habitat	Black paper	5	15	25
	Newspaper	20	5	20
	White paper	25	15	5

6. Sample answer: The data supported our hypothesis because fewer prey are found on backgrounds of the same color, and more prey are found when the background is a contrasting color.

7. Sample answer: The more similar the prey color is to its habitat, the fewer the number of prey that will be captured. Therefore, a predator will find prey more easily when its prey is a color that does not match its habitat.

QUICK LAB GUIDED Inquiry

Prey Coloration

In this lab, you will develop and run an experiment to test how well different prey animals evade capture by a predator.

PROCEDURE

1 Work with a partner to establish three different habitats using the sheets of paper provided. If possible, spread the paper on a table or desk. Otherwise, lay the pieces of paper on the floor.

2 The small paper circles represent prey. Assign one student to play the role of the predator. Start with the black paper. Scatter 15 of each type of the paper circles on the black paper. What procedure could you follow to test how well any of the prey evade capture by the predator?

_____

_____

_____

3 Repeat Step 2 for the white paper as your habitat, then the newsprint.

4 Think about your model and what it will show. Then, finish the hypothesis statement below.
More prey animals survive when their coloring is _____ the coloring of their environment because predators _____

_____ .

5 Carry out your experiment, recording your findings in a table that you construct in the space below.

OBJECTIVE
• Investigate how predator efficiency is affected by prey coloration.

MATERIALS
For each pair
• cups to hold paper circles (3)
• paper, black, 8.5 × 11
• paper, newsprint, 8.5 × 11
• paper, white, 8.5 × 11
• paper circles, black
• paper circles, newsprint
• paper circles, white
• stopwatch

Quick Lab continued

6 Evaluate your results in light of the hypothesis you completed in Step 4. Do your results support your hypothesis? Explain.

_____

_____

_____

7 What can you conclude about the relationship between prey color, habitat color, and how these factors affect the ability of a predator to capture its prey?

_____

_____

_____

QUICK LAB GUIDED Inquiry

Identifying Predators and Prey BASIC

👥 Student pairs

🕐 20 minutes

LAB RATINGS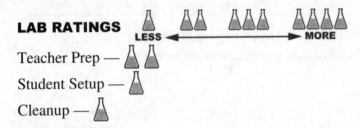

Teacher Prep —

Student Setup —

Cleanup —

TEACHER NOTES

In this activity, students work in pairs to identify characteristics of organisms based on their roles as predators or prey. For example, a tiger's binocular vision enhances its ability to locate prey and so this characteristic is related to its role as a predator. A mouse has sensitive hearing, which enhances its ability to avoid being eaten as prey. Some animals have a mix of both predator and prey characteristics.

Tip This activity will help students understand that characteristics of organisms suit them to particular ecological roles such as predator or prey.

Student Tip Think about how different animals sense their environment in different ways and what characteristics help them detect other animals.

Skills Focus Classifying Examples, Constructing Tables, Comparing Features

MODIFICATION FOR DIRECTED Inquiry

Provide a blank data table for students at the same time you give them the images to analyze.

MATERIALS

For each pair

Images (from online search)

- chameleon
- crocodile
- deer
- hawk
- housefly
- lion
- moth
- mouse
- praying mantis
- salmon
- spider
- tiger
- other images as appropriate

My Notes

_____

_____

_____

_____

_____

Answer Key

1. Accept all reasonable answers. Students may base their sorting on their own knowledge of the behaviors of these animals.

2. Accept all reasonable answers. Sample answers:

Example	Predator	Prey	Relevant physical characteristics
chameleon	✓	✓	camouflage, rotating eyes, long tongue
crocodile	✓		strong teeth and jaws, lies in wait
deer		✓	eyes either side of head, dull colors, horizontal eye pupils
hawk	✓		ability to fly, binocular vision, strong talons and beak
housefly		✓	ability to fly, fast moving, lack of jaws
lion	✓		binocular vision, strong teeth and jaws, vertical eye pupils
moth		✓	camouflage, ability to fly
mouse		✓	dull coloration, eyes either side of head
praying mantis	✓	✓	strong jaws, lies in wait, binocular vision
salmon	✓	✓	fast swimmer, schooling behavior
spider	✓	✓	forms a web, various colors
tiger	✓		binocular vision, strong teeth and jaws, vertical eye pupils

3. Accept all reasonable answers. Sample answer: Predators have specialized characteristics that allow them to locate prey, such as binocular vision, which allows estimation of distance.

4. Accept all reasonable answers. Sample answer: Prey animals have sensory organs that alert them to potential predators.

Identifying Predators and Prey

In this lab you will review characteristics of various animals and use those characteristics to identify the animals as predator or prey or both.

PROCEDURE

1 Your teacher will give you several images of animals. Look over the images with your partner and sort them into groups depending on whether you think they act as predators, prey, or both. Write down what reasoning you used to sort the animals into groups.

_____

_____

_____

_____

2 Study each image and identify the physical characteristics of the animal shown that help it either capture prey (if it is a predator) or evade predators (if it is a prey animal). Keep in mind some may be both. Make a table to summarize your identifications for each image. Be sure your table includes everything you have identified for each animal. Make your table in the space below.

OBJECTIVE

- Investigate characteristics of animals to identify adaptations that help them survive in their roles as predators or prey.

MATERIALS

For each pair
Images (from online search)

- chameleon
- crocodile
- deer
- hawk
- housefly
- lion
- moth
- mouse
- praying mantis
- salmon
- spider
- tiger
- other images as appropriate

Quick Lab continued

❸ What similarities or differences do you notice about the predators?

_____

_____

_____

❹ What similarities or differences do you notice about the prey?

_____

_____

_____

EXPLORATION LAB GUIDED *Inquiry* **AND** INDEPENDENT *Inquiry*

Modeling the Predator-Prey Cycle GENERAL

👥 Student pairs

🕐 45 minutes

LAB RATINGS

LESS ◄————————► MORE

Teacher Prep —

Student Setup —

Cleanup —

MATERIALS

For each pair
- bean bags (optional)
- cardboard squares, 5 cm × 5 cm (20)
- cardboard squares, 1 cm × 1 cm (100)
- paper, graphing
- pencil
- table top, about 75 cm × 75 cm

My Notes

_____

_____

_____

_____

_____

TEACHER NOTES

The aim of this activity is to demonstrate a classic predator-prey cycle. When predator numbers go up, prey numbers go down, and vice versa. Over time, there is a cycle so that predators and prey are in balance. The student is challenged to simulate the interaction between predator and prey following simple rules. During each generation, the student attempts to "catch" the prey with the "predator." The prey squares are distributed randomly on the table top. The student throws the predator square on the table and prey touching the predator square are deemed to be "caught." Emphasize that the squares only need to land safely near the prey on the table inside the work area. For each prey not caught, three new prey squares are added to the next generation. With successive generations, the prey population increases. The predator population increases in response. Over time, the prey population decreases and the predator population increases. Eventually predators will cease catching prey. The predator population will decrease, and the prey population will increase, beginning the cycle again. If tables are not available, students can perform this activity on the floor.

Tip This activity will help students understand the relationship between predators and prey in nature.

Student Tip Consider what happens to prey populations when predators are few, and vice versa.

Skills Focus Modeling Nature, Analyzing Concepts, Drawing Conclusions

MODIFICATION FOR DIRECTED *Inquiry*

For the directed inquiry option, give an exact number for prey to reproduce rather than provide a range as in the Guided Inquiry option or use any number as in the independent inquiry option. Bean bags can be used as an optional material to cardboard squares.

Answer Key for GUIDED Inquiry

MAKE OBSERVATIONS

6. Sample data:

		A	B	C	D	= A-D	= 2D	= 3C
		Starting number of predators	Starting number of prey	Number of prey remaining	Number of successful predators	Number of failed predators	Ending number of predators*	Ending number of prey**
Generations	1	2	10	4	2	0	4	12
	2	4	12	3	3	1	6	9
	3	6	9	3	2	4	4	9
	4	4	9	3	2	2	4	9
	5	4	9	6	1	3	2	18
	6	2	18	15	1	1	2	45
	7	2	45	39	2	0	4	100
	8	4	100	88	4	0	8	100
	9	8	100	82	6	2	12	100
	10	12	100	88	4	8	8	100
	11	8	100	79	7	1	14	100
	12	14	100	76	8	6	16	100
	13	16	100	70	10	6	20	100
	14	20	100	82	6	14	12	100
	15	12	21	14	5	7	10	42

7. Sample answer: The number of generations will be represented on the *x*-axis. Predator and prey numbers will be represented on the *y*-axis.

ANALYZE THE RESULTS

8. Sample answer: Over time the predator and prey populations varied. When the prey population increased, the predator population increased.

Connect TO THE ESSENTIAL QUESTION

9. Sample answer: Populations are expected to cycle over time. The populations may not cycle if the predator or prey dies out. The system's behavior is very sensitive to the starting conditions.

Answer Key for INDEPENDENT Inquiry

MAKE OBSERVATIONS

2. Sample answer: The smaller squares represent prey.

3. Sample answer: The larger squares represent predators. Removal of the small squares represents predators eating the prey.

4. Accept all reasonable answers.

5. Sample answer: The number of new prey squares added per prey remaining represents the prey reproductive rate. This addition represents the prey population reproducing and its next generation (iteration).

Sample answer: The limit on the number of prey represents the habitat's carrying capacity.

7. Answers will vary. Sample data:

		A	B	C	D	= A-D	= 2D	= 3C
		Starting number of predators	Starting number of prey	Number of prey remaining	Number of successful predators	Number of failed predators	Ending number of predators*	Ending number of prey**
Generations	**1**	2	10	4	2	0	4	12
	2	4	12	3	3	1	6	9
	3	6	9	3	2	4	4	9
	4	4	9	3	2	2	4	9
	5	4	9	6	1	3	2	18
	6	2	18	15	1	1	2	45
	7	2	45	39	2	0	4	100
	8	4	100	88	4	0	8	100
	9	8	100	82	6	2	12	100
	10	12	100	88	4	8	8	100
	11	8	100	79	7	1	14	100
	12	14	100	76	8	6	16	100
	13	16	100	70	10	6	20	100
	14	20	100	82	6	14	12	100
	15	12	21	14	5	7	10	42

Exploration Lab continued

8. Sample answer: The number of generations will be represented on the *x*-axis. Predator and prey numbers will be represented on the *y*-axis.

ANALYZE THE RESULTS

9. Sample answer: Over time the predator and prey populations varied. When the prey population increased, the predator population also increased because there was a lot of available food. As the predators caught more prey, the prey population decreased. With decreased amounts of prey (food), the predator population decreases. This allows the prey population to rebound and the cycle starts all over again. If there are too few prey, the predator dies out.

10. Sample answer: This model system differs from a real system in several ways:
- Reproductive rate of animals is variable. In this system, we used a consistent rate.
- Most natural systems have many more individuals.
- Death can be caused by many factors, not just predators.
- The number of generations in natural systems is indefinite.
- Predators and prey evolve, so prey get better at avoiding predators, and predators get better at catching prey.

Connect TO THE ESSENTIAL QUESTION

11. Sample answer: Populations are expected to cycle over time. The populations may not cycle if the predator or prey dies out. The system's behavior is very sensitive to the starting conditions.

Modeling the Predator-Prey Cycle

In this lab, you will model predator-prey populations to determine if there is a relationship between the populations over time.

PROCEDURE

ASK A QUESTION

1 In this lab, you will investigate the following question: How are predator-prey populations linked?

MAKE OBSERVATIONS

2 Take ten small cardboard squares and distribute them randomly on the table top. These squares represent prey. Toss three large cardboard squares in the air above the table and see where they land. These are the predators.

3 Remove any of the small squares that the larger square touches. The small squares that you remove represent prey eaten by the predator. Count the remaining prey squares on the table and enter this number in the data table on the next page. Record the number of successful predators (any which touched a prey square). Fill in the rest of the table for Generation 1.

OBJECTIVE

- Investigate how populations of predator and prey vary to result in a predator-prey population cycle.

MATERIALS

For each pair

- bean bags (optional material)
- cardboard squares, 5 cm × 5 cm (20)
- cardboard squares, 1 cm × 1 cm (100)
- paper, graphing
- pencil
- table top, about 75 cm × 75 cm

Exploration Lab continued

		A	B	C	D	= A-D	= 2D	= 3C
		Starting number of predators	Starting number of prey	Number of prey remaining	Number of successful predators	Number of failed predators	Ending number of predators*	Ending number of prey**
Generations	1	3	10					
	2							
	3							
	4							
	5							
	6							
	7							
	8							
	9							
	10							
	11							
	12							
	13							
	14							
	15							

* This number = the ending number of predators. Use this number in Column A for the next generation.
** This number = the ending number of prey. Use this number in Column B for the next generation.

Before Beginning Generation 2:

❹ For every prey square remaining on the table, add either two, three, or four new prey squares to the table. Decide on the number you would like to use and stick with that number throughout this lab. This addition represents the prey population's next generation. For every predator that caught prey, add one more predator card to the table. This addition represents the predator population's next generation.

Exploration Lab continued

5 Keep in mind that every population has a carrying capacity: the environment can only support a certain population of each type of organism. The carrying capacity for your prey will be 100, so if your prey reaches that number you cannot add any more to the table. The carrying capacity of your predators will be ten.

6 If a predator did not catch a prey square, do not use it in the next throw. (For example, if two of your predator cards caught prey, you would use a total four cards as predators in the next throw.) Write the new starting number of predators in the table for Generation 2. Throw the predator cards again.

6 Repeat Steps 3 through 5 for 15 generations.

7 When you have completed 15 generations, graph your data on graphing paper. What quantity will be on the *x*-axis? What quantity will be on the *y*-axis?

_____

_____

ANALYZE THE RESULTS

8 **Recognizing Patterns** What do you observe about the numbers of predators and prey over time? Do you see any patterns or predictable behavior? If not, why not?

_____

_____

_____

Connect TO THE ESSENTIAL QUESTION

9 **Applying Concepts** Given the codependence of predator and prey, how do their populations vary over time?

_____

_____

_____

_____

_____

_____

_____

_____

EXPLORATION LAB INDEPENDENT Inquiry

Modeling the Predator-Prey Cycle

In this lab, you will model predator-prey populations to find if there is a relationship between the populations over time.

PROCEDURE

ASK A QUESTION

1 In this lab, you will investigate the following question: How are predator-prey populations linked?

MAKE OBSERVATIONS

2 Take ten small cardboard squares and distribute them randomly on the table top. What do these squares represent?

_____

3 Take three of the larger squares and throw them in a random direction on the table. Remove any of the small squares that the larger square touches. What do the larger squares represent? What does removal of the small squares represent?

_____

4 Count the remaining prey squares and enter this number in the data table.

OBJECTIVE

• Investigate how populations of predator and prey vary to result in a predator-prey population cycle.

MATERIALS

For each pair

• cardboard squares, 5 cm × 5 cm (20)

• cardboard squares, 1 cm × 1 cm (100)

• paper, graphing

• pencil

• table top, about 75 cm × 75 cm

Exploration Lab continued

		A	B	C	D	= A-D	= 2D	= 3C
		Starting number of predators	Starting number of prey	Number of prey remaining	Number of successful predators	Number of failed predators	Ending number of predators*	Ending number of prey**
Generations	1	3	10					
	2							
	3							
	4							
	5							
	6							
	7							
	8							
	9							
	10							
	11							
	12							
	13							
	14							
	15							

* This number = A for the next generation. ** This number = B for the next generation.

5 For each "prey" remaining on the table, decide how many new prey squares to add to the table. What does this number represent?

_____

Make sure that you add the same multiple of new squares per remaining square. Experiment with using different multiples of new prey squares. If needed, add cards up to the maximum 100 possible. What does this limit represent?

_____

Exploration Lab continued

6 For each predator that caught an item, add another predator card. If a predator did not catch a prey, do not use it in the next throw. (For example, if two of your predator cards caught prey, you would use a total four cards as predators in the next throw.) Write the total number of predators in the table. Throw the predator cards again.

7 Repeat Steps 3–6 for 15 generations.

8 When you have completed 15 generations, graph your data on graphing paper. What quantity will be on the *x*-axis? What quantity will be on the *y*-axis?

_____

_____

ANALYZE THE RESULTS

9 **Recognizing Patterns** What do you observe about the numbers of predators and prey over time? Do you see any patterns or predictable behavior? If not, why not?

_____

_____

_____

10 **Comparing Systems** How does this model system differ from a real system?

_____

_____

_____

Connect TO THE ESSENTIAL QUESTION

11 **Applying Concepts** Given the codependence of predator and prey, how do their populations vary over time?

_____

_____

_____

_____

_____

_____

QUICK LAB **DIRECTED** *Inquiry*

Climate Determines Plant Life GENERAL

👥 Individual student

🕐 20 minutes

LAB RATINGS

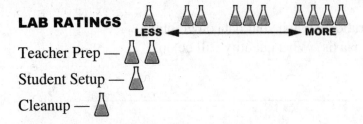

LESS ◄──────────► MORE

Teacher Prep —

Student Setup —

Cleanup —

MATERIALS

For each student

- cactus, small, potted
- lab apron
- markers or colored pencils
- nonsucculent house plant, small, potted
- safety goggles

SAFETY INFORMATION

Remind students to review all safety cautions and icons before beginning this lab.

TEACHER NOTES

In this activity, students will analyze the relationship between plant features and climate. You may want to provide supplemental images of cacti and house plants. Cactus plants are easy to maintain and generally need limited space. For this activity, provide a cactus growing in sand. The nonsucculent house plant should be growing in standard, moist potting mix. For the house plant, a pothos ivy is slow-growing and requires little care; an African violet is also recommended.

Student Tip Think about how roots support plants and take in nutrients from the soil.

Skills Focus Making Observations, Making Predictions, Applying Concepts

My Notes

_____

_____

_____

_____

_____

MODIFICATION FOR INDEPENDENT *Inquiry*

Provide students with a description of a climate and have them develop a model of a plant that grows well in the climate. Have students present their completed models to the class.

Quick Lab continued

Answer Key

2. Sample answer: The African violet has "furry" leaves; the cactus has no leaves. (Some students might know that spines are modified leaves.) The cactus might be able to hold more water than the African violet because its body is thick and bulbous.

3. Sample answer: The water disappeared quickly into the sandy soil. The water soaked into already moist soil of the nonsucculent plant more slowly. The water beaded up on the surfaces of both kinds of plants.

4. Answers may vary.

5. Students may know or infer that cactuses come from dry climates and nonsucculents tend to come from less dry climates.

Climate Determines Plant Life

In this lab, you will compare and contrast characteristics of plants from different climates.

◆◆◆◆◆

PROCEDURE

① Observe the **cactus** and the nonsucculent **house plant.**

② Write down at least four observations about each plant. Are the stems and leaves of the two plants similar? How do they differ? Are both green? Do both seem to hold a large volume of water? Do both have defenses against animals that would eat them?

_____

_____

_____

_____

_____

_____

_____

_____

_____

③ With an eye dropper, drop several drops of water onto the surface of each plant and onto the soil in which it is growing. Does the water behave differently on the different soils? On the different plants?

_____

_____

_____

_____

_____

OBJECTIVES

• Compare and contrast plant structures.

• Describe the relationship between plant features and climate.

MATERIALS

For each student

• cactus, small, potted
• lab apron
• markers or colored pencils
• nonsucculent house plant, small, potted
• safety goggles

Quick Lab continued

4 Draw two pictures showing what you think the roots of each plant are like.

5 Describe the climate that most likely supports each plant. Explain why each plant is suited for that particular climate.

_____

_____

_____

_____

_____

_____

_____

_____

_____

_____

_____

_____

QUICK LAB GUIDED *Inquiry*

Identify Your Land Biome GENERAL

👥 Small groups
🕐 30 minutes

LAB RATINGS

LESS ◄——————► MORE

Teacher Prep —

Student Setup —

Cleanup —

MATERIALS

For each group

• computer with Internet access or field guide of local plants

• pencil

My Notes

_____

_____

_____

_____

_____

TEACHER NOTES

In this activity, students will work in small groups to discuss what they know about the local environment. Based on prior knowledge, they will predict the land biome found where they live. Then, students will use approved reference materials (field guides and websites) to research the predominant species in the local plant community and the average annual climate data. Using this information, students will evaluate their prediction to arrive at a more informed understanding of the biome in which they live.

Nearby county, state, and national parks are good sources of information on native plant and animal life. The National Oceanic and Atmospheric Administration (NOAA) and the National Weather Service (NWS) are good sources of climate data.

Tip This activity will help students identify prior knowledge and test their predictions by researching facts.

Student Tip Think about the plants such as trees, shrubs, and grasses that grow naturally in the place where you live.

Skills Focus Making Predictions, Analyzing Data, Drawing Conclusions

MODIFICATION FOR INDEPENDENT *Inquiry*

Present students with the task of predicting the biome in which they live. Then ask them to suggest the types of information they could research to help them determine whether their prediction was accurate. Allow them to proceed with reasonable plans for research.

Quick Lab continued

Answer Key

1. Answer will vary.

2. Answers will vary.
   Teacher Prompt What trees, shrubs, or grasses are most common?

3. Answers will vary.

4. Answers will vary.

5. Sample answer: No, because the trees I thought were native are actually introduced species.

6. Accept all reasonable answers.

QUICK LAB GUIDED *Inquiry*

Identify Your Land Biome

In this lab, you will predict the major land biome in which you live. You will then gather climate data and information about the main plant types found in your local area to decide whether your prediction was accurate.

PROCEDURE

❶ With your lab group, discuss the major land biomes that are found on Earth. Decide which biome is present where you live. Record your prediction.

We live in the _____ biome.

❷ Look up the names of four native plants that are very common where you live. Use only sources such as a field guide or a website approved by your teacher. Record the name and type of each plant. (Example: Sugar maples are deciduous trees.)

_____

_____

❸ Look up the average annual high and low temperatures and rainfall amount for where you live. Use only sources approved by your teacher. Record the data you find. Then use the data to make graphs of the average temperatures and rainfall amounts for each month of the year.

_____

_____

OBJECTIVES

• Predict the biome in which you live.
• Describe the dominant plant community in your area.
• Describe climate factors (average temperature and rainfall) for your area.

MATERIALS

For each group
• computer with Internet access or field guide of local plants
• pencil

Graphs of Monthly Average Temperatures and Rainfall Amounts per Year

Quick Lab continued

4 Compare the results of your research with the descriptions of the land biomes in your textbook. Which land biome best fits your data? _____

5 Did your conclusion match your prediction? Explain why or why not.

_____

_____

6 How does the climate where you live affect the plant community that grows there?

_____

_____

_____

Survey of a Biome's Biotic and Abiotic Factors GENERAL

👥 Small groups

🕐 Three 45-minute class periods

LAB RATINGS

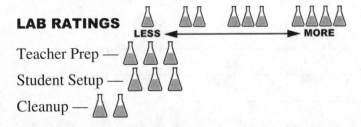

LESS ◄────────► MORE

Teacher Prep —

Student Setup —

Cleanup —

MATERIALS

For each group
- binoculars
- camera
- colored pencils
- computer with Internet access
- drawing paper
- field notebook
- garden shovel
- light meter
- local field guides (plants, animals, soils)
- magnifying lens
- plastic bags
- ruler, metric

For each student
- protective clothing
- protective gloves

SAFETY INFORMATION

Remind students to review all safety cautions and icons before beginning this lab. Have students pay particular attention to the guidelines for safety in field investigations. Students should wear protective clothing and gloves when handling any plants. Be sure students know which plants and animals they might encounter are harmful and that students can identify these organisms. Advise students to avoid all contact with these organisms. You may wish to survey the intended area(s) of study prior to conducting the activity to make sure no dangerous plants and/or animals are in the area.

TEACHER NOTES

In this activity, students will work in small groups to research biotic and abiotic factors in their local ecosystem. Then students will use the information in planning activities for a field investigation. If a suitable natural area is not convenient to the school, make arrangements to take students to a nearby city or county park for their field investigation. Identify websites that provide useful information about local plant and animal life and average climate data. Nearby county, state, and national parks are good sources of information on native plant and animal life. The National Oceanic and Atmospheric Administration (NOAA) and the National Weather Service (NWS) are good sources of climate data.

Tip This activity will guide students in preparing for and carrying out a field investigation. If observation of a natural ecosystem is not possible, have students create a small ecosystem in their classroom or school vicinity and monitor changes in the abiotic and biotic factors over time. The following sites have useful information:

http://ezinearticles.com/?Self-Contained-Micro-Ecosystem-in-a-Fish-Tank&id=2911055

www.carolina.com/category/teacher+resources/classroom+activities/the+river+tank+-+a+versatile+tool.do

www.kidsgardening.com/growingideas/projects/june04/pg1.html

My Notes

_____

_____

_____

_____

_____

Field Lab continued

Student Tip As you work in the field, you will probably notice something that surprises you. Examples might be a kind of plant that is very abundant or is blooming, a rock with interesting colors or patterns, an area of very deep shade, or a huge and colorful caterpillar. Based on your research, such discoveries are not likely to be one of the factors you expected to find.

Skills Focus Classifying Samples, Analyzing Data, Drawing Conclusions

MODIFICATION FOR DIRECTED Inquiry

Rather than having students research climate data, provide this information for them.

Answer Key for GUIDED Inquiry

RESEARCH A PROBLEM

4. Answers will vary.

DEVELOP A PLAN

5. Answers will vary.

6. Sample answer: Cool damp weather is predicted. We should dress in warm, waterproof clothing, wear sturdy waterproof shoes, and take rain gear along in case it is needed.

MAKE OBSERVATIONS

8. Answers will vary and should be recorded in a field notebook.

9. Answers will vary and should be recorded in a field notebook.

10. Answers will vary and should be recorded in a field notebook.

ANALYZE THE RESULTS

12. Answers will vary.

13. Sample answer: The soil samples all tested as being sandy.

14. Sample answer: Areas that had less light had more plant cover, and areas with the most light had no plants shading the area.

15. Sample answer: No; a possible reason is that the only area we could study outside was not natural anymore.

Connect TO THE ESSENTIAL QUESTION

17. Sample answer: The data we collected helped us describe some of the characteristics of the biome where we live.

Answer Key for INDEPENDENT Inquiry

RESEARCH A PROBLEM

4. Answers will vary.

Field Lab continued

DEVELOP A PLAN

5. Accept all reasonable answers.

6. Sample answer: Cool damp weather is predicted. We should dress in warm, waterproof clothing, wear sturdy waterproof shoes, and take rain gear along in case it is needed.

MAKE OBSERVATIONS

8. Answers will vary.

ANALYZE THE RESULTS

9. Sample answer: No; a possible reason is that the only area we could study outside was not natural anymore.

10. Sample answer: Plants use light to grow. Areas that had less light had more plant cover, and areas with the most light had no plants shading them.

11. Sample answer: The light meter was used to take readings of the amount of light reaching the ground in several different areas. The shovel and plastic bags were used for collecting soil samples.

13. Sample answer: The soil samples all tested as being sandy.

Connect TO THE ESSENTIAL QUESTION

15. Sample answer: The data we collected helped us describe some of the characteristics of the biome where we live.

FIELD LAB GUIDED *Inquiry*

Survey of a Biome's Biotic and Abiotic Factors

In this lab, you will collect data on biotic and abiotic factors in an outdoor area. Before you go outside, you will do some research about the kinds of biotic and abiotic factors that should be found in the biome where you live. In the field, you will make observations and record them with a camera. You will collect a handful of soil to observe and test in your classroom or lab. You may even collect samples of insects to identify back at school. You will then organize the information in a report.

PROCEDURE

ASK A QUESTION

1 In this lab, you will investigate the following question: What are some of the biotic and abiotic factors found in the biome in which you live?

RESEARCH A PROBLEM

2 Use the field guides provided by your teacher to learn about the plants, animals, and soil types in the area where you live. Identify several plants and animals you think you might see while you are in the field. Record their names and the information you learn about each one in the table below.

Name of organism	Brief description (How will you know it if you see it?)	Role in the ecosystem (producer, consumer, decomposer)	Poisonous or Dangerous (Yes or No)

OBJECTIVES

- Investigate biotic and abiotic factors in the biome in which you live.
- Summarize characteristic biotic and abiotic factors of a biome.

MATERIALS

For each group
- binoculars
- camera
- colored pencils
- computer with Internet access
- drawing paper
- field notebook
- garden shovel
- light meter
- local field guides (plants, animals, soils)
- magnifying lens
- plastic bags
- ruler, metric

For each student
- protective clothing
- protective gloves

Field Lab continued

3 Find out what kinds of poisonous plants and dangerous animals you are likely to find (if any). Be sure you know what each one looks like so you can avoid handling it in the field.

4 Identify the average climate data for the area where you live. Your teacher will suggest a website that will contain data for the following:

-Average High Temperature: _____

-Average Low Temperature: _____

-Average Mean Temperature: _____

-Average Precipitation: _____

-Average Number of Sunny Days: _____

-Average Number of Cloudy Days: _____

DEVELOP A PLAN

5 Discuss with your group what each person will do as you collect samples and data in the field. Decide what each person will do and which of the lab's materials that person will need. Each group will need one person for each of the following jobs:

-making observations of biotic factors: _____

-making observations of abiotic factors: _____

-recording observations by making notes and illustrations in a field notebook and taking pictures with a camera: _____

6 Find out what kind of weather is forecast for the day you will be in the field. Describe what kind of weather you expect and how you will dress for the day.

_____

_____

_____

MAKE OBSERVATIONS

7 Collect the tools and equipment you will use in the field before you leave. Take care to avoid disturbing the natural environment as you work.

Field Lab continued

8 Try to locate at least three kinds of the plants your group expects to find. Also try to locate at least one plant not listed in the table above as well. **CAUTION: Do not touch any part of a poisonous plant you find.** Examine and describe each plant's leaves as well as its flowers and seeds, if possible. Wear protective gloves to observe and measure the parts of the plants. Record observations in words and pictures (photos or illustrations) in your notebook. If you do not find plants that your group expected to find, observe others.

9 Try to locate at least three kinds of the animals your group expects to find. Also locate at least one animal not listed in the table above as well. **CAUTION: Do not touch or approach any animal you find.** Examine each kind of animal you find at a safe distance. Observe what the animal looks like, what it is eating (if anything), and its behavior. Record observations in words and pictures (photos or illustrations) in your notebook. If you do not find animals that your group expected to find, observe others.

10 In at least three different areas, use the light meter to take readings of the amount of light (in lux). Record the values in your field notebook. Describe in your field notebook the plant cover in the locations where light-meter readings are taken. For example, if no leaves are over the area, it has no plant cover. If the area is under the canopy of a tree, there will be heavy plant cover.

11 Put on protective gloves. Use the garden shovel and plastic bags to collect a handful of soil from at least three different areas. Collect only from areas with bare soil. Do not disturb the roots of plants by digging too deeply.

ANALYZE THE RESULTS

12 **Examining Samples** Use the field guides to identify any unknown plants or animals your group observed. What additional plants and animals did you find in the field?

_____

_____

_____

13 **Examining Samples** Wet the soil samples you collected with a small amount of tap water. Squeeze each sample in a gloved hand. Observe what happens to the ball of soil when the hand opens. If it all sticks together, it is mostly clay. If it completely falls apart, it is mostly sand. If it breaks apart in clumps, it is a kind of soil called loam. Were all the soil samples you collected the same? Explain.

_____

_____

_____

Field Lab continued

14 **Analyzing Data** How did the density of plants relate with the readings taken with the light meter? Explain any trend you observed.

_____

_____

_____

15 **Evaluating Results** Did you find all the plants and animals you expected to find? Explain why or why not.

_____

_____

_____

DRAW CONCLUSIONS

16 **Organizing Observations** Summarize the information you discovered about your local ecosystem in a written or online report with illustrations.

Connect TO THE ESSENTIAL QUESTION

17 **Identifying Patterns** How will the data you collected in this investigation help you identify the biome in which you live? What is the name of the biome where you live?

_____

_____

_____

FIELD LAB INDEPENDENT *Inquiry*

Survey of a Biome's Biotic and Abiotic Factors

In this lab, you will collect data on biotic and abiotic factors in an outdoor area. Before you go outside, you will do some research about the kinds of biotic and abiotic factors that should be found in the biome where you live. In the field, you will make observations and record them with a camera. You will collect a handful of soil to observe and test in your classroom or lab. You may even collect samples of insects to identify back at school. You will then organize the information in a report.

PROCEDURE

ASK A QUESTION

❶ In this lab, you will investigate the following question: What are some of the biotic and abiotic factors found in the biome in which you live?

RESEARCH A PROBLEM

❷ Use the materials provided by your teacher to identify and describe some of the biotic and abiotic factors in your local area. You will use this information to plan and carry out a field investigation of a local ecosystem. Identify several plants and animals you think you might see while you are in the field. Record their names and the information you learn about each one in the table below.

Name of organism	Brief description (How will you know it if you see it?)	Role in the ecosystem (producer, consumer, decomposer)	Poisonous or Dangerous (Yes or No)

OBJECTIVES

- Investigate biotic and abiotic factors in the biome in which you live.
- Summarize characteristic biotic and abiotic factors of a biome.

MATERIALS

For each group
- binoculars
- camera
- colored pencils
- computer with Internet access
- drawing paper
- field notebook
- garden shovel
- light meter
- local field guides (plants, animals, soils)
- magnifying lens
- plastic bags
- ruler, metric

For each student
- protective clothing
- protective gloves

Field Lab continued

3 Find out what kinds of poisonous plants and dangerous animals you are likely to find. Be sure you know what each one looks like so you can avoid handling it in the field.

4 Identify the average climate data for the area where you live. Your teacher will suggest a website that will contain data for the following:

-Average High Temperature: _____

-Average Low Temperature: _____

-Average Mean Temperature: _____

-Average Precipitation: _____

-Average Number of Sunny Days: _____

-Average Number of Cloudy Days: _____

DEVELOP A PLAN

5 Brainstorm with other members of your group. Decide which biotic and abiotic factors you will study. Include observations of plants, animals, soil, and amount of light in your investigation. Plan how you will make observations in a nearby park or natural area. Include steps you should take before going into the field. Also identify safety concerns and how they will be handled. Write the steps of your plan below.

_____

_____

_____

_____

6 Find out what kind of weather is forecast for the day you will be in the field. Describe what kind of weather you expect and how you will dress for the day.

_____

_____

Field Lab continued

MAKE OBSERVATIONS

7 Collect the materials you will use in the field before you leave. Take care to avoid disturbing the natural environment as you work.

8 Record your observations in an organized manner.

ANALYZE THE RESULTS

9 **Examining Samples** Use the field guides to identify any unknown plants or animals observed. While in the field, did you find any plants and animals you did not expect to find? What were they?

_____

_____

10 **Defending Methods** Explain why you were asked to find the average climate data for the area where you live.

_____

_____

11 **Describing Methods** How did you use the light meter in your investigation? How did you use the garden shovel and plastic bags?

_____

_____

12 **Applying Methods** Use the following procedure to learn more about the soil in your area. Wet the soil samples you collected with a small amount of tap water. Squeeze each sample in a gloved hand. Observe what happens to the ball of soil when the hand opens. If it all sticks together, it is mostly clay. If it completely falls apart, it is mostly sand. If it breaks apart in clumps, it is a kind of soil called loam.

13 **Interpreting Results** Were all the soil samples you collected the same? Explain.

_____

_____

_____

Field Lab continued

DRAW CONCLUSIONS

14 **Organizing Observations** Summarize the information you discovered about your local ecosystem in a written or online report with illustrations.

Connect **TO THE ESSENTIAL QUESTION**

15 **Identifying Patterns** How will the data you collected in this investigation help you identify the biome in which you live? What is the name of the biome where you live?

_____

_____

_____

QUICK LAB DIRECTED *Inquiry*

Life in Moving Water ADVANCED

👥 Small groups

🕐 20 minutes

LAB RATINGS

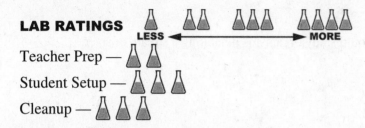

LESS ← → MORE

Teacher Prep —

Student Setup —

Cleanup —

SAFETY INFORMATION

Remind students to review all safety cautions and icons before beginning this lab. Sand and soil can cause eye damage. Students should wear goggles at all times while handling sand and soil.

TEACHER NOTES

In this activity, students will explore adaptations useful for life in moving water. If available, you could add an aquarium pump that agitates different parts of the model differently. This effect could be mimicked by a water faucet or pouring a jug of water into the model. Students will then be able to see how rocks, nooks, and crannies create different niches.

Student Tip Try changing the angle of the pan as you tilt it. How does this affect the ground material?

Skills Focus Making Models, Drawing Conclusions, Developing Procedures

MODIFICATION FOR INDEPENDENT *Inquiry*

Students should research a specific stream or river niche. Based on their research, students should develop a model of an organism that is suited for life in a stream or river. Students can present their completed models to the class. Models can be drawings, computer generated images, or 3-dimensional sculptures.

MATERIALS

For each group
- bowl
- cup
- pan, rectangular
- small suction cups
- substrates (pebbles, rocks, sand, and/or soil) to be used as ground material
- water

For each student
- gloves
- lab apron
- safety goggles

My Notes

_____

_____

_____

_____

_____

Answer Key

3. Sample answer: The ground material is moving and changing because it is washed downstream by the water.

4. Accept all reasonable answers.

5. Accept all reasonable answers.

6. Accept all reasonable answers.

   Teacher Prompt Consider how you could study organisms inhabiting a stream or river.

QUICK LAB DIRECTED *Inquiry*

Life in Moving Water

Streams and rivers are bodies of water that move at different speeds, ranging from very slow and calm to fast and turbulent.

PROCEDURE

1 Firmly attach a few suction cups to the bottom surface of the pan. Then carefully arrange larger rocks and then smaller rocks on the bottom of the pan. Pour substrate (small pebbles, sand, or soil) to a depth of about 1 in.

2 Tilt the pan over the **bowl.** Pour the **cup of water** into the top end of the pan.

3 What happens to the ground material as the water flows down the pan?

_____

_____

_____

_____

_____

_____

4 What organisms might live in an ecosystem like this? Do you think they are mobile (able to move freely) or sessile (unable to move freely)?

_____

_____

_____

_____

_____

_____

OBJECTIVES

• Model a stream or river niche.

• Describes adaptations useful for life in moving water.

MATERIALS

For each group
• bowl
• cup
• pan, rectangular
• small suction cups
• substrates (pebbles, rocks, sand, and/or soil) to be used as ground material
• water

For each student
• gloves
• lab apron
• safety goggles

Quick Lab continued

❺ What did the suction cups represent? In the space below, draw pictures of two different adaptations you think organisms may use to fasten themselves to the soil or to rocks in moving water.

❻ Suggest one way that you could investigate how realistic your ideas for adaptations are.

_____

_____

_____

_____

_____

_____

_____

_____

QUICK LAB **GUIDED Inquiry**

Light Penetration and Water Clarity **GENERAL**

MATERIALS

For each pair of students
- beakers, large (2)
- coins, shiny (2)
- flashlight
- flour
- paper, dark
- stirring stick, wooden or spoon
- water

👥 Student pairs
🕐 20 minutes

LAB RATINGS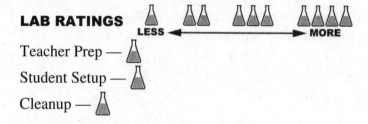

Teacher Prep —

Student Setup —

Cleanup —

My Notes

_____
_____
_____
_____
_____

SAFETY INFORMATION

Remind students to review all safety cautions and icons before beginning this lab. Keep paper towels on hand, and be sure that students wipe up any water that spills. Have them wash and dry their hands upon completion of this activity.

TEACHER NOTES

In this activity, students predict the effect of water clarity on light penetration into water. They will then test their predictions with a simple experiment and make an inference about how water clarity may affect an ecosystem. A film of flour may form on the surface of the water. Use a paper towel to blot it off.

Student Tip Compare a clear pond and a muddy pond. How is your ability to see to the bottom of each pond different?

Skills Focus Making Predictions, Describing Observations, Making Inferences

MODIFICATION FOR **INDEPENDENT Inquiry**

Present students with the problem and then give them the materials they can use to test their prediction. This will give students the opportunity to make their own procedure rather than following a set method.

As an alternative method for measuring turbidity, have students write their name on a piece of paper with permanent marker, tape the paper to the bottom of the beaker, add water, add flour, stir gently, and determine when they can no longer read their name when they shine a flashlight into the water.

Another possibility is to place a light-powered calculator beneath the beaker and determine how much flour must be added so that the calculator can no longer function.

Quick Lab continued

Answer Key

1. Sample answer: I think that clear water will let more light pass through it.

6. Sample answer: In the beaker with clear water, the light on the coin was bright. In the beaker with added flour, the water looked cloudy, the light spread out and looked softer, and the coin could not be seen.

7. Sample answer: The particles in the cloudy water blocked some of the light from reaching the bottom of the beaker.

8. Sample answer: An aquatic ecosystem with cloudy water would have fewer producers, or the producers would not make as much food and would support fewer consumers.

QUICK LAB GUIDED *Inquiry*

Light Penetration and Water Clarity

Some natural waters, including streams and ponds, have very clear water. Others have cloudy (or turbid) water. The cloudiness is caused by the amount and kind of matter mixed with the water. In this lab, you will predict how water clarity affects light passing through an aquatic ecosystem and use an experiment to test your prediction.

PROCEDURE

1 Discuss the importance of sunlight on food chains and food webs. Brainstorm with your partner about how clear water and cloudy water might affect the sunlight that enters a body of water. Record your prediction.

_____

_____

2 Fill two large beakers with water. Place both on the dark sheet of paper. Drop a shiny coin into each one.

3 Add a small amount of the flour to one beaker and stir.

4 Shine the flashlight into each beaker from the top. Observe the appearance of the water, the light, and the coins.

5 Draw each beaker and your observations of its contents in the space below. Include a way to show how the light behaves in your sketch.

OBJECTIVES

- Compare the amount of light penetration in clear water with that in cloudy water.
- Describe how water clarity might affect living things in an aquatic ecosystem.

MATERIALS

For each pair of students
- beakers, large (2)
- coins, shiny (2)
- flashlight
- flour
- paper, dark
- stirring stick, wooden or spoon
- water

Quick Lab continued

6 What differences did you observe between the two water samples?

_____

_____

7 Explain what happened to the light in the cloudy water.

_____

_____

8 How might the food chains in an aquatic ecosystem be affected by cloudy water?

_____

_____

_____

QUICK LAB DIRECTED Inquiry

Pyramid of Energy GENERAL

👥 Individual student
🕐 10 minutes

LAB RATINGS

LESS ← → MORE

Teacher Prep —
Student Setup —
Cleanup —

MATERIALS

For each student
- colored pencils, red, blue, and green
  (1 of each color)

My Notes

_____

_____

_____

_____

_____

TEACHER NOTES

In this activity, students will examine the sources of energy in an ecosystem and the balance of producers with consumers.

Student Tip If you had an unusually small meal for dinner, think about lunch or another recent meal that is typical for you.

Skills Focus Organizing Data, Drawing Conclusions

MODIFICATION FOR INDEPENDENT Inquiry

Ask students to explore what types of events cause imbalances in the relationships between consumers and producers (drought, disease, etc). Have students formulate an explanation based on their research. Students should then create a model that communicates their explanation. Students should include both quantitative and qualitative data as support.

Answer Key

6. Sample answer: Toward the top of the food pyramid, less food (and hence energy) remains available for the next level.

    Teacher Prompt When an herbivore eats plants, where does all that energy go? Sample answer: Most of the energy is lost to the environment.

7. Most students will place themselves at the top of the pyramid as secondary consumers. Vegetarians will place themselves near the middle as primary consumers.

8. Sample answer: All pyramids show a greater number of producers than consumers.

9. Sample answer: Food provides energy for the body. It also is a source for molecular building blocks for cellular structure.

Pyramid of Energy

In this activity, you will study how energy moves through an ecosystem.

PROCEDURE

1 In the top row of the table below, list all of the foods you ate for dinner last night.

2 Below each food item, write down where the energy in that food came from. For example: milk came from a cow and salad came from a lettuce plant.

3 If you have written any consumers in that row, again list where the energy came from. For example, a cow's energy comes from grass.

4 Continue this process until all of the columns end in producers or decomposers.

OBJECTIVES

- Create a personal energy pyramid.
- Describe the relationship between consumers and producers.

MATERIALS

For each student

- colored pencils, red, blue, and green (1 of each color)

MY ENERGY PYRAMID

Quick Lab continued

5 Shade all producers in green and all consumers in red. If you ate decomposers, shade them in blue.

6 Why are there more producers than consumers?

_____

_____

_____

_____

_____

_____

_____

7 Re-examine your paper. Where would you place yourself in this energy pyramid?

_____

8 Look at some of the other students' pyramids. How do they compare to yours?

_____

_____

_____

_____

_____

_____

_____

9 How is food used by your body?

_____

_____

_____

QUICK LAB INDEPENDENT *Inquiry*

Model the Carbon Cycle GENERAL

👥 Small groups

🕐 25 minutes

LAB RATINGS

LESS ←————————→ MORE

Teacher Prep —

Student Setup —

Cleanup —

MATERIALS

For each group
- paper
- pencils
- other materials as requested by students (e.g., cardboard, construction paper, glue, marbles, plastic cups, glitter)

TEACHER NOTES

In this lab, students will model the movement of carbon from one reservoir to another in the carbon cycle. Guide students in brainstorming the reservoirs in the carbon cycle. Collect any requests for materials, and assist students in obtaining materials needed for their models. Invite students to share their models with the class, and ask students to evaluate the strengths and limitations of different models.

Student Tip Your model could illustrate the carbon cycle (for example, a diorama or detailed diagram). It could also be a model that shows the flow of carbon through the cycle (for example, using marbles to represent carbon, cups or other containers to represent reservoirs, and chutes or slides to show how the carbon moves between the reservoirs). Be creative!

Skills Focus Making Models, Evaluating Models

My Notes

_____

_____

_____

_____

_____

MODIFICATION FOR GUIDED *Inquiry*

Have students create a game to model the movement of carbon from one reservoir to another in the carbon cycle. Students can choose the type of game to use, but each game should include information about specific reservoirs and processes.

Answer Key

1. Sample answers:

Reservoir	Processes by which carbon moves into the reservoir
carbonate rocks	carbon-rich sediment from the shells of marine organisms collects on the bottom of the oceans
living things	consumers consume other living things; producers take in carbon from the atmosphere
atmosphere	respiration from living things, burning fossil fuels, volcanoes
soil	decay of once-living things
fossil fuels	burial of the remains of once-living things

4. Accept all reasonable responses.

5. Accept all reasonable responses.

Model the Carbon Cycle

In this lab, you will create a model to show how carbon moves from one reservoir to another in the carbon cycle. A reservoir is any place on Earth where a certain material is found.

PROCEDURE

1 Brainstorm a list of reservoirs in the carbon cycle. Write the major reservoirs in the chart below. Then, complete the chart by adding a description of the process or processes by which carbon moves into each reservoir.

Reservoir	Processes by which carbon moves into the reservoir

OBJECTIVE

- Construct a model to show how matter moves continuously in the carbon cycle.

MATERIALS

For each group

- paper
- pencils
- other materials as needed

Quick Lab continued

2 Plan your model. Sketch or briefly describe your plan on a separate sheet of **paper.** Be sure your model will include a way to represent the movement of materials from one reservoir to another. Submit a request for any materials you need to your teacher.

3 When your teacher has approved your plan, construct your model and present it to the class. Be sure to clearly label or describe all parts of the model.

4 Analyze the different models of the carbon cycle. Discuss the strengths and limitations of each model.

_____

_____

_____

_____

_____

_____

_____

_____

5 Write an evaluation of your own model on the lines below. Describe the strengths and limitations of your model. Identify ways you could improve your model.

_____

_____

_____

_____

_____

_____

_____

QUICK LAB DIRECTED *Inquiry*

Condensation and Evaporation GENERAL

👥 Individual student

🕐 5 minutes one day, plus 15 minutes a second day

LAB RATINGS

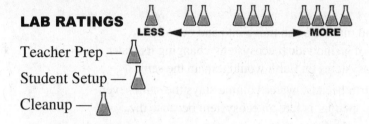

LESS ◀——————▶ MORE

Teacher Prep —

Student Setup —

Cleanup —

SAFETY INFORMATION

Remind students to review all safety cautions and icons before beginning this lab.

TEACHER NOTES

In this activity, students will observe the processes of condensation and evaporation and make connections to open and closed systems. Water loss for the open jar will be greatest in hot, dry conditions. If you have a cool, humid climate and no heat lamp, you may want to wait several days before re-measuring. Transparent plastic cups can be substituted for the jars.

Skills Focus Making Models, Applying Concepts

MODIFICATION FOR INDEPENDENT *Inquiry*

To understand changing environmental factors, students could brainstorm ways in which the water volume in an environment could be affected. Ask students to generate a list of variables that would help them extend and refine their models.

MATERIALS

For each student
- jars, clear unbreakable
- lab apron
- measuring cup
- plastic wrap
- rubber band
- water
- safety goggles

My Notes

_____

_____

_____

_____

_____

Answer Key

4. Accept all reasonable answers.

5. Accept all reasonable answers.

6. Sample answer: The open jar had less water the next day, but the closed jar contained the same amount. The water escaped from the open jar but did not escape from the closed jar.

7. Sample answer: An ecosystem is open and materials can move into and out of an ecosystem. Water can move into and out of an individual ecosystem, changing its water volume. The total water volume in all ecosystems on Earth would remain the same.

8. Sample answer: The closed jar is like Earth because water volume stays the same, even though the water can change forms. The open jar is like an ecosystem because the water volume can change as water moves in and out of the ecosystem.

9. Sample answer: Water volume in the open jar could be affected by temperature and humidity in the air.

QUICK LAB DIRECTED *Inquiry*

Condensation and Evaporation

In this activity, you will observe how condensation and precipitation affect the mass of water in a system.

PROCEDURE

1 Pour exactly 1 cup of **water** into each of two **jars.**

2 Cover one jar with **plastic wrap** and seal tightly with a **rubber band.**

3 Place both jars in a sunny location or under a heat lamp and leave overnight.

4 The next day, record your observations about both jars in the space below.

_____

_____

_____

_____

5 Gently tap the plastic wrap covering the first jar to knock any condensation back into the jar. Then, remove the plastic wrap and measure the volume of water in each jar.

Volume in Jar 1: _____ Volume in Jar 2: _____

6 Was there a difference in water volume when you measured the second time? Why or why not?

_____

_____

_____

_____

_____

OBJECTIVES
- Describe the processes of condensation and evaporation.
- Describe the difference between open and closed systems.

MATERIALS
For each student
- jars, clear unbreakable
- lab apron
- measuring cup
- plastic wrap
- rubber band
- water
- safety goggles

Quick Lab continued

7 Does water volume change on Earth? Does it change in an individual ecosystem?

_____

_____

_____

_____

_____

_____

8 How was the closed jar like Earth? How is the open jar like an ecosystem?

_____

_____

_____

_____

_____

_____

9 What factors might affect water volume in the open jar?

_____

_____

_____

_____

_____

_____

_____

QUICK LAB DIRECTED Inquiry

Measuring Species Diversity GENERAL

👥 Individual student

🕐 10 minutes

LAB RATINGS

LESS ◄————► MORE

Teacher Prep —

Student Setup —

Cleanup —

MATERIALS

For each student
• paper
• pencil

My Notes

_____

_____

_____

_____

_____

TEACHER NOTES

In this activity, students will calculate a biodiversity index of a sample region. They will also read a graph of biodiversity indices to interpret changes in populations over time. The biodiversity index is a comparison of the number of living organisms to the number of species in a given area. It is an important indicator of how biologically active a particular geographic region is and whether it is in danger of over-specialization. For example, a 1-meter square area of lawn with 100 organisms, including 5 species of worms, 7 species of insects, and 3 species of millipedes, would have a biodiversity index of $(5 + 7 + 3)/100 = 0.15$. Biodiversity indices are discrete for species of plants or animals. Plant and animal species should not be combined during the calculations.

Skills Focus Applying Concepts, Drawing Conclusions

MODIFICATION FOR GUIDED Inquiry

Instead of providing students with sample data, ask them to calculate the biodiversity index for a known region of their choice that contains multiple species of either plants or animals. Students should create a procedure for recording data and turn in their data and calculations as a lab report.

MODIFICATION FOR INDEPENDENT Inquiry

Ask students to research populations of species for a region of their choice and then calculate the biodiversity index (for either plants or animals) for that region. Students should create a procedure for research and data collection before beginning the activity, and turn in their data and calculations as a lab report when they are finished.

Answer Key

2. Sample answer: There are 24 organisms and 4 species, so BI is 4/24 = 0.2.

3. Sample answer: There is a parasite-host relationship among the ticks and the horses and cats. All of the organisms are consumers. There is a predator-prey relationship among the cats and mice.

4. Sample answer: The index declined by half, so the region lost half its diversity in 25 years.

QUICK LAB DIRECTED *Inquiry*

Measuring Species Diversity

In this lab, you will calculate the biodiversity index for a sample region. You will also read a graph of the change in biodiversity index over time to determine the change in species populations over time.

PROCEDURE

1 Use your **pencil** and **paper** to answer the following questions.

2 A barn contains 2 horses, 10 ticks, 2 cats, and 10 mice. What is the biodiversity index for this region?

_____

_____

3 What specific relationships (predator/prey, consumer/producer, or parasite/host) most likely occur between these species?

_____

_____

_____

OBJECTIVES

- Calculate the biodiversity index of a sample region.
- Interpret a graph to determine the change in biodiversity over time.

MATERIALS

For each student

- paper
- pencil

113

Quick Lab continued

4 The graph below shows the biodiversity index for a freshwater habitat. What can you conclude about the change in the number of species from 1960 to 1985?

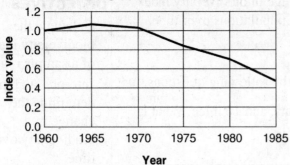

Measuring Species Diversity

Source: www.unepwcmc. org/information_services/
publications/freshwater/3.htm

_____

_____

_____

_____

Investigate Evidence of
Succession GENERAL

👥 Student pairs
🕐 30 minutes

LAB RATINGS

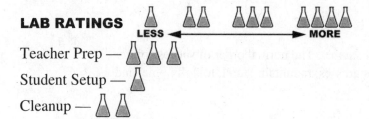

Teacher Prep —

Student Setup —

Cleanup —

MATERIALS

For teacher prep
- glass beads
  (4 colors)
- sand, coarse and dry
- stopper or screw-on
  cap (to fit each test
  tube)
- test tubes, large
  (2 or 3 per group)

For each group
- model soil cores
  (2 or 3)

For each student
- safety goggles

SAFETY INFORMATION

Remind students to review all safety cautions and icons before beginning
this lab.

TEACHER NOTES

In this activity, students will work in pairs to examine model soil core
samples from a fictional oak climax forest. They will observe the
predominant type of pollen found in each level of the sample. Then, students
will use their observations to infer the changes in the kinds of plants present
as the site underwent succession. Prepare the model soil cores by filling test
tubes with coarse sand mixed with beads of four different colors to represent
pollen of grass, mountain laurel (a woody shrub), loblolly pine, and oak.
Make a key that shows which color of bead represents each plant species.
Place 3–4 centimeters (cm) of sand mixed with beads of the color for grass
pollen in the bottom of each test tube. Repeat using sand mixed with beads
of the color for mountain laurel pollen and then loblolly pine pollen,
respectively. Place 3–4 cm of sand mixed with beads of the color for oak
pollen at the top of each test tube. Seal the test tubes with corks or screw-on caps.

Tip This activity may help students understand the process of observing a soil core for
evidence of different kinds of plants. Prepare three or four sets of cores that consist of one
core from an undisturbed area (showing the normal succession of species) and one or two
cores from disturbed areas (with beads in a non-normal order, such as those for grass pollen
between two layers of mountain laurel pollen to show that the process of succession started
over). Pairs of students can take turns making observations of each of the class sets.

Student Tip Think about the layers that form in a flowerbed as people add soil and mulch
and plants drop leaves and seeds over time. The soil in a forest builds up over time, due to
the deposition of dust and plant material on the soil surface. Older layers always lie beneath
younger layers.

Skills Focus Making Observation, Interpreting Results, Inferring Events

My Notes

_____

_____

_____

_____

_____

MODIFICATION FOR INDEPENDENT *Inquiry*

Have students research different types of disturbances that interrupt the process of succession. Then, have them build models that represent how these disturbances would be reflected in studies of pollen or seeds found in soil cores.

Answer Key

1. Sample answer: Based on the presence of four different colors of beads, we saw four different layers.

2. Accept all reasonable answers.

3. Answers will vary depending on the soil sample. The normal order of succession for the four kinds of plants used in the lab is grasses, mountain laurel, loblolly pine, and oak.

4. Accept all reasonable answers.

QUICK LAB GUIDED *Inquiry*

Investigate Evidence of Succession

In this lab, you will examine model soil core samples from a fictional climax oak forest. Over time, plants spread to new areas while they die out in other areas. As plants live and die, they leave behind pieces of themselves that become part of the soil. Therefore, the soil contains a record of how the plant community on a plot of land has changed over time. Ecologists use soil core samples to observe plant structures that do not easily break down, such as seeds and pollen grains. The kinds of plants represented by your model pollen grains are oak trees, loblolly pine trees, mountain laurel shrubs, and grasses.

PROCEDURE

1 Observe the model soil cores your teacher has prepared. Describe what you see in each model.

_____

_____

_____

_____

2 Draw the layers you can see in each soil core based on differences in the colors of the beads (model pollen grains). Use the key to identify which pollen grain color symbolizes which plant when you label the kind of pollen found in each layer.

OBJECTIVES

- Examine soil core samples from a climax forest.
- Observe differences in pollen content at successive levels in the core sample.
- Relate changes in pollen type to stages of succession in the forest's past.

MATERIALS

For each group:
- model soil cores (2 or 3)

For each student
- safety goggles

Quick Lab continued

❸ Use the model soil cores to infer the order in which the four types of plants grew.

_____

_____

❹ Based on your knowledge of succession, identify the soil cores in which the normal order of succession was disturbed. Justify your answers.

_____

_____

_____

FIELD LAB `GUIDED Inquiry` **AND** `INDEPENDENT Inquiry`

Predicting How Succession Follows a Human Disturbance GENERAL

MATERIALS

For each student
• paper
• pencils, colored

🔬 Individual student
🕐 Two 45-minute periods

LAB RATINGS

LESS ⬅➡ MORE

Teacher Prep —
Student Setup —
Cleanup —

My Notes

_____
_____
_____
_____
_____

SAFETY INFORMATION

Be sure students use care to choose a safe place to sit as they make their sketches. Students should be asked to wash their hands after their field experience.

TEACHER NOTES

In this activity, students will observe an area outdoors that has been heavily developed by humans. They will record their observations in a drawing. Then, students will imagine how the area would change over time if humans no longer occupied Earth. Encourage students to use their imaginations as well as their knowledge of the processes of change on Earth. They will make a total of four sketches to show how the area will change over the next 200 years.

Tip This activity enables students to practice making predictions about what changes will occur in the future, based on their knowledge of natural processes that occur on Earth. It will also enable those with drawing ability to shine. Choose a location near the school that contains a large proportion of cement, asphalt, or other human-made surface.

Student Tip Tell students who are reluctant to draw that the content of their drawings is most important, not the quality of the art. Explain that both individuals with knowledge and critical thinking skills and individuals with creative skills play important roles in the practice of science.

Skills Focus Making Predictions, Constructing Drawings, Applying Patterns

MODIFICATION FOR `DIRECTED Inquiry`

Have class discussions to allow students to exchange ideas about the types of changes they might expect to see at each time point. Allow students to make their drawing for that time point following the class discussion pertaining to that time point.

Answer Key for GUIDED Inquiry

FORM A PREDICTION

2. Accept all reasonable answers.

ANALYZE THE RESULTS

8. Sample answer: grasses, weeds, and wildflowers.

9. Sample answer: Wind, birds, and other animals brought seeds of grasses and wildflowers into the cracks in the asphalt and concrete.

10. Sample answer: bushes and woody shrubs.

11. Sample answer: Weathering by plant roots and climate factors will break down the asphalt and concrete. More soil will form in the area, and the wind, water, and animals will bring in seeds of different kinds of plants.

12. Sample answer: different shrubs and trees.

13. Sample answer: Continued weathering by plant roots and climate factors, as well as erosion and deposition of soil, will make more soil. The wind and animals will bring in the seeds of trees and different shrubs that will be able to grow in the changed environment.

DRAW CONCLUSIONS

14. Sample answer: secondary succession; because it began in an area where plants had grown before but were destroyed by humans as they developed the land.

15. Sample answer: by observing disturbed areas nearby that have been undergoing succession for different periods of time.

Connect TO THE ESSENTIAL QUESTION

16. Sample answer: When the natural environment is destroyed, the natural processes of weathering and secondary succession rebuild the ecosystem. Weathering creates soil, and wind and animals bring in seeds of plants. Pioneer plants begin to grow first and help change the abiotic factors in the ecosystem. The changes in the ecosystem make it possible for different types of plants to grow. Eventually, a climax community will form.

Answer Key for INDEPENDENT Inquiry

FORM A PREDICTION

2. Accept all reasonable answers.

ANALYZE THE RESULTS

8. Sample answer: grasses, weeds, and wildflowers.

9. Sample answer: Wind, birds, and other animals brought seeds of grasses and wildflowers into the cracks in the asphalt and concrete.

Field Lab continued

10. Sample answer: bushes and woody shrubs.

11. Sample answer: Weathering by plant roots and climate factors will break down the asphalt and concrete. More soil will form in the area, and the wind, water, and animals will bring in seeds of different kinds of plants.

12. Sample answer: different shrubs and trees.

13. Sample answer: Continued weathering by plant roots and climate factors, as well as erosion and deposition of soil, will make more soil. The wind and animals will bring in the seeds of trees and different shrubs that will be able to grow in the changed environment.

DRAW CONCLUSIONS

14. Sample answer: secondary succession; because it began in an area where plants had grown before but were destroyed by humans as they developed the land.

15. Sample answer: by observing disturbed areas nearby that have been undergoing succession for different periods of time.

Connect TO THE ESSENTIAL QUESTION

16. Sample answer: When the natural environment is destroyed, the natural processes of weathering and secondary succession rebuild the ecosystem. Weathering creates soil, and wind and animals bring in seeds of plants. Pioneer plants begin to grow first and help change the abiotic factors in the ecosystem. The changes in the ecosystem make it possible for different types of plants to grow. Eventually, a climax community will form.

Predicting How Succession Follows a Human Disturbance

In this activity, you will show how natural processes might change the parts of Earth's surface developed by humans. No structure built by humans can stay the same forever. Developments such as shopping centers stay in good condition as long as humans take care of them. Once humans abandon a development, nature begins to reclaim it through the processes of weathering, erosion, and succession. You will start by observing an area outdoors that has been heavily developed by humans. You will record your observations in a drawing. Then, you will imagine how the area would change over time if humans were no longer around. Using your knowledge of succession, you will make three more sketches to show how the area will change over the next 200 years.

OBJECTIVE

- Use knowledge of the concept of primary succession to predict long-term changes in an abandoned human development.

MATERIALS

For each student
- paper
- pencils, colored

PROCEDURE

ASK A QUESTION

1 In this lab, you will investigate the following question: How will an area developed by humans change after humans are no longer there?

FORM A PREDICTION

2 Write a prediction that answers the question above. Make sure your statement includes the word "because."

_____

_____

_____

Field Lab continued

MAKE OBSERVATIONS

3 Sit in one location, designated by your teacher, and observe the way humans have changed the area in the process of development. In the space below, make a detailed drawing of what you see. You may make your drawing on a separate piece of paper. Label the main parts of your drawing. (Examples: Asphalt parking lot, concrete sidewalk, brick wall, flowerbed)

MAKE PREDICTIONS

4 Imagine that people no longer live in the place that you drew. Think about how, over time, natural processes such as weathering and succession will affect the structures you labeled.

5 Make a drawing of how the place will look in 10 years based on your knowledge of weathering and succession. Label the new organisms that will be found in the area.

Field Lab continued

6 Make a drawing of how the place will look in 50 years, based on your knowledge of weathering and succession. Label the new organisms that will be found in the area.

7 Make a drawing of how the place will look in 200 years, based on your knowledge of weathering and succession. Label the new organisms that will be found in the area.

ANALYZE THE RESULTS

8 **Identifying Patterns** What kinds of pioneer species did you add to your second drawing?

_____

_____

_____

Field Lab continued

9 **Explaining Concepts** How will the pioneer species be able to start growing in the developed area after 10 years?

_____

_____

_____

_____

10 **Identifying Patterns** What kinds of plants and animals did you add to your drawing of the area after 50 years?

_____

_____

_____

11 **Explaining Concepts** How will the different plants and animals be able to establish populations in the area after 50 years?

_____

_____

_____

_____

12 **Identifying Patterns** What kinds of plants and animals did you add to your drawing of the area after 200 years?

_____

_____

_____

13 **Explaining Concepts** How will the different plants and animals be able to establish populations in the area after 200 years?

_____

_____

_____

_____

_____

Field Lab continued

DRAW CONCLUSIONS

14 **Forming Conclusions** Which type of succession do your drawings show?
Justify your answer.

_____

_____

_____

15 **Defending Predictions** How could you defend the prediction you made
and developed in your drawings?

_____

_____

_____

_____

_____

Connect TO THE ESSENTIAL QUESTION

16 **Describing Patterns** How will the parts of an ecosystem that are destroyed
by human development change over time?

_____

_____

_____

_____

FIELD LAB **INDEPENDENT** *Inquiry*

Predicting How Succession Follows a Human Disturbance

In this activity, you will show how natural processes might change the parts of Earth's surface. You will start by observing an area outdoors that has been destroyed by a natural process such as a flood or has been heavily developed by humans. You will record your observations in a drawing. Then, you will imagine how the area would change over time without the influence of humans. Using your knowledge of succession, you will make three more sketches to show how the area will change over the next 200 years.

PROCEDURE

ASK A QUESTION

❶ In this lab, you will investigate the following question: How will an area developed by humans change after humans are no longer there?

FORM A PREDICTION

❷ Write a prediction that answers the question above. Make sure your statement includes the word "because."

_____

_____

_____

OBJECTIVE
• Use knowledge of the concept of primary succession to predict long-term changes in an abandoned human development.
MATERIALS
For each student
• paper
• pencils, colored

Field Lab continued

MAKE OBSERVATIONS

3 Sit in one location of your choice, and observe the way it looks after a natural disaster or development by humans has changed it. In the space below, make a detailed drawing of what you see. You may make your drawing on a separate piece of paper. Label the main parts of your drawing. (Examples: Asphalt parking lot, concrete sidewalk, flowerbed, bare soil, gully)

MAKE PREDICTIONS

4 Imagine that people will have no effect on the place that you drew. Think about how natural processes such as weathering and succession will affect the structures you labeled over time.

5 Make a drawing of how the place will look in 10 years based on your knowledge of weathering and succession. Label the new organisms that will be found in the area.

Field Lab continued

6 Make a drawing of how the place will look in 50 years, based on your knowledge of weathering and succession. Label the new organisms that will be found in the area.

7 Make a drawing of how the place will look in 200 years, based on your knowledge of weathering and succession. Label the new organisms that will be found in the area.

ANALYZE THE RESULTS

8 **Identifying Patterns** What kinds of pioneer species did you add to your second drawing?

_____

_____

_____

Field Lab continued

9 **Explaining Concepts** After 10 years, what will foster the growth of the pioneer species in the developed area?

_____

_____

_____

_____

10 **Identifying Patterns** What kinds of plants and animals did you add to your drawing of the area after 50 years?

_____

_____

11 **Explaining Concepts** How will the different plants and animals be able to establish populations in the area after 50 years?

_____

_____

_____

_____

12 **Identifying Patterns** What kinds of plants and animals did you add to your drawing of the area after 200 years?

_____

_____

13 **Explaining Concepts** How will the different plants and animals be able to establish populations in the area after 200 years?

_____

_____

_____

_____

Field Lab continued

DRAW CONCLUSIONS

⑭ Forming Conclusions Which type of succession do your drawings show?
Justify your answer.

_____

_____

_____

⑮ Defending Predictions How could you defend the prediction you made
and developed in your drawings?

_____

_____

_____

_____

_____

Connect TO THE ESSENTIAL QUESTION

⑯ Describing Patterns How will the parts of an ecosystem that are destroyed
by natural events or by human development change over time?

_____

_____

_____

_____

_____

Biodiversity All Around Us GENERAL

👥 Small groups
🕐 40 minutes

LAB RATINGS

LESS ← → MORE

Teacher Prep —

Student Setup —

Cleanup —

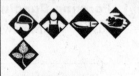

MATERIALS

For each group
• flashlight
• magnifying glass
• meterstick
• string, 4 m in length
For each student
• lab apron
• safety goggles

SAFETY INFORMATION

Remind students to review all safety cautions and icons before beginning this lab. Contact with certain plants and animals may cause injury or allergic reactions. Students should use caution while outside and should wash their hands at the end of the lab. Advise students to report broken flashlights or magnifying glasses immediately so that you can clean up any pieces of glass.

TEACHER NOTES

In this activity, students will explore how environmental factors and human activity impact ecosystems. Survey the areas that students propose to observe to make sure they do not contain harmful plants. Adult supervision is recommended while students are making their observations. This lab could be extended to a field trip that involves parents. If you are unable to take students on a field trip, help them understand the difference between a severely disturbed area (a paved parking lot) and an area that is less disturbed (a natural area). Different levels of biodiversity exist everywhere.

Skills Focus Making Observations, Applying Concepts

MODIFICATION FOR GUIDED Inquiry

Lead students on a tour of the grounds outside your school. Ask them to describe their surroundings and identify areas where they would expect higher and lower levels of biodiversity. Challenge students to think of how they could assess biodiversity. Allow students to conduct all reasonable experiments. When students have collected and analyzed their data, have groups compare their results to determine how biodiversity changed with location.

My Notes
_____
_____
_____
_____
_____

Quick Lab continued

Answer Key

1. Answers will vary.
3. Answers will vary.
4. Answers will vary.

QUICK LAB DIRECTED Inquiry
Biodiversity All Around Us

In this lab, you will observe the biodiversity of an area and identify the relationships among various organisms.

PROCEDURE

❶ As a group, select a site outside where you will observe and measure biodiversity. Describe the area you chose. Do you see evidence of human activity? Do you expect your area to have high biodiversity? Why or why not?

_____

_____

_____

_____

_____

_____

_____

_____

_____

_____

_____

_____

❷ Within the site you chose, use a **meterstick** and **string** to measure and mark off a 1 m² area. Use a **magnifying glass** and **flashlight** to carefully inspect the area you marked.

OBJECTIVES
- Measure the biodiversity of a specific area.
- Identify relationships among organisms.

MATERIALS
For each group
- flashlight
- magnifying glass
- meterstick
- string, 4 m in length

For each student
- lab apron
- safety goggles

Quick Lab continued

❸ List all the different organisms you observe within your area. Count and record the number of each organism. If you cannot identify an organism, indicate that it is different (for example, list "plant A" and "plant B").

_____

_____

_____

_____

_____

_____

_____

_____

❹ What kinds of relationships do you think exist among the organisms you observed? List any examples you saw of producers, consumers, predators, prey, parasites, mutualism, commensalism, and competition.

_____

_____

_____

_____

_____

_____

_____

_____

_____

_____

_____

_____

_____

_____

QUICK LAB DIRECTED Inquiry

Investigate the Acidity of Water GENERAL

👥 Student pairs

🕐 20 minutes

LAB RATINGS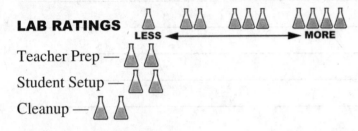

Teacher Prep —

Student Setup —

Cleanup —

MATERIALS

For each pair
• containers, plastic (3)
• marker
• paper, graphing
• paper, pH
• water sample, bottled
• water sample, pond, lake, or stream (depending on availability)
• water sample, rainwater (recently collected)
• water sample, tap

For each student
• lab apron
• safety goggles

SAFETY INFORMATION

Remind students to review all safety cautions and icons before beginning this lab. Because this lab may involve outside activity, remind students to use care when moving about natural areas that may be uneven or slippery. Also tell students that the pH paper is impregnated with chemicals that are potentially toxic. Students should not touch the paper to their skin (especially if they want to test their saliva).

TEACHER NOTES

In this activity, students will collect water from various sources and test each sample for acidity. If possible, have students collect water directly from natural sources. Back in the classroom, student pairs will sample a minimum of three readily available sources of water: tap water, bottled water, and rainwater. The students add each of the water samples to a separate clean, dry container. The student then uses the pH paper to estimate the pH (acidity) of the samples. It is best to place a small drop of water on the pH paper than to dip the paper into the water. Results are best when short range pH paper (3.0–7.0) or similar is used. If needed, the teacher directs students on how to estimate pH by comparing color changes in the pH paper to a standard chart.

In general, water pH can vary depending on its source; rainwater is often more acidic than other water sources. Students will discover that the pH of tap and bottled water are similar and close to 7. The rainwater pH will be lower. The student will determine whether the rainwater sample indicates acid rain. The student will create a bar chart to compare the acidity of the samples.

Tip Engage the student by explaining that the acidity of water varies depending on its source and that this difference can have environmental and health consequences.

Skills Focus Following Procedures, Drawing Conclusions, Presenting Data

MODIFICATION FOR GUIDED Inquiry

Have students determine their own procedure given the same listed set of materials.

My Notes

_____

_____

_____

_____

_____

Answer Key

5. Accept all reasonable answers.

6. Accept all reasonable answers. Students should make a graph that reflects their data.

7. Sample answer: The acidity varies in the samples of water. Tap and bottled water have a pH of around 7. Rainwater is more acidic with a pH of around 5.5.

8. Accept all reasonable answers. Students may conclude that their sample of rainwater is indicative of acid rain because its pH is lower than tap or bottled water. However, normal rainwater pH is around 5.5. Acid rain has a lower pH on the order of 4.5.

9. Accept all reasonable answers. Students should recognize that other substances may be dissolved in the water. Those substances may affect the characteristics of water even though they cannot be seen.

QUICK LAB DIRECTED *Inquiry*

Investigate the Acidity of Water

Freshwater is present in our environment in many different places. There are natural sources of freshwater such as rivers, lakes, streams, and ponds. Rain, snow, and sleet/hail represent another type of water source. Then there are the sources that we use every day such as tap water and bottled water.

   Does water from all of these sources differ? If so, how does it differ? In this lab, you will explore the acidity of various water samples to see how it varies depending on its source. You will be able to use that information to determine whether any of the natural water sources have been negatively affected by human activities.

PROCEDURE

❶ Collect water from a variety of sources. Be sure that you have at least three samples that include tap water, bottled water, and rainwater.

❷ Add a sample of the tap water to one of the containers.

❸ Use the marker pen to label the sample. Use an abbreviation if you don't have enough space (e.g., TW).

❹ Repeat Steps 2 and 3 for each of the water samples labeling each sample appropriately.

❺ Dip a cotton swab into one of the water samples and use it to transfer a small drop of water to a piece of pH paper. Use the color indicator key on the package of pH paper to determine the approximate pH of the water. Write down your findings. Then repeat with the remaining samples.

_____

_____

_____

❻ Use graph paper to present your results as a bar chart.

OBJECTIVE

• Determine the acidity of a variety of water samples and create a bar chart to present your results.

MATERIALS

For each pair
• containers, plastic (3)
• marker
• paper, graphing
• paper, pH
• water sample, bottled
• water sample, pond, lake, or stream (depending on availability)
• water sample, rainwater (recently collected)
• water sample, tap
For each student
• lab apron
• safety goggles

Quick Lab continued

7 What can you conclude about differences in acidity between the different water samples?

_____

_____

_____

8 Acid rain is a type of precipitation produced when air pollutants enter the water cycle. The pH of acid rain is on the order of 4.5. Does your rainwater sample suggest that acid rain is a problem in your area? Explain.

_____

_____

_____

9 Why do you think the pH of water can vary from source to source?

_____

_____

_____

FIELD LAB `GUIDED Inquiry` **AND** `INDEPENDENT Inquiry`

Field Investigation of Plant Quantity and Diversity GENERAL

👥 Small groups

⏱ Three 45-minute class periods

LAB RATINGS

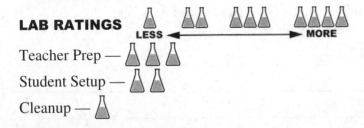

LESS ◀——————▶ MORE

Teacher Prep —

Student Setup —

Cleanup —

MATERIALS

For each group
- field notebook
- map of local area
- plant identification key (optional)
- wire square quadrat, 30 cm × 30 cm

For each student
- protective clothing suitable for field study

SAFETY INFORMATION

Remind students to review all safety cautions and icons before beginning this lab. This lab requires outside activity. Because this lab involves outside activity, students should be cautioned to use care when moving about natural areas that may be uneven or slippery. Be sure students are aware of harmful plants they might encounter and advise students to avoid all contact with them.

My Notes

_____

_____

_____

_____

_____

TEACHER NOTES

In this activity, students observe differences in plant quantity and diversity between two different local sites. Areas such as lawns, golf courses, nature reserves, parks, city lots, or agricultural land may be used. Students work in groups to assess the plant diversity and quantity present within a standard area of 30 centimeters (cm) × 30 cm. The group will determine what kinds of sites to investigate and how many samples are needed to get a representative sample of the number of different types of plants growing in the sampled area. At each of the sites, students will:

- Count the number of plant species present.
- Estimate plant cover versus bare ground for each sample.

Students will determine a plan for collecting data by developing their own data tables before heading out into the field. Students will develop their own procedure and make their own conclusions based on their results.

Wire squares (quadrats) can be made by bending coat hangers into a 30 cm × 30 cm square.

Tip This lab requires three full class periods to complete. Some time needs to be allowed for students to get to the sites they have chosen for study. One option is to limit their choices to areas within close walking distance of your school.

Student Tip How can the wire square help you to find as many plant species as possible in a specific area?

Skills Focus Collecting Data, Calculating Results, Drawing Conclusions

Field Lab continued

MODIFICATION FOR DIRECTED Inquiry

Provide students with pre-selected sites to study. (A larger space may be necessary for study, depending on the space available at your school.) Also provide them with data tables to use as they conduct their field study. You may also wish to provide them with separate keys for different types of plants.

Answer Key for GUIDED Inquiry

ASK A QUESTION

1. Sample answer: How do humans impact the quantity and diversity of plants living in an area?

Teacher Prompt Consider the ways humans use land and how that may affect the different kinds of plants that grow in a particular area.

FORM A PREDICTION

2. Accept all reasonable answers.

Teacher Prompt What types of events would have a negative impact on plants growing in an area and who is responsible for causing those events?

MAKE A PLAN

3. Accept all reasonable answers.

Teacher Prompt How are your sites used by people?

4. Accept all reasonable answers. Students' data tables should include space for repeated sampling. A sample table is shown:

			Data and Observations		
		Trial #	Number of plant species found	Plant cover	Observations and notes
Type of land use	Lawn	1			
		2			
		3			
		4			
	Vacant lot	1			
		2			
		3			
		4			

ANALYZE THE RESULTS

11. Accept all reasonable answers. Check that students have made the correct calculation from their data.

Field Lab continued

DRAW CONCLUSIONS

12. Accept all reasonable answers. Be sure that students' conclusions are consistent with the data they collected.

Connect **TO THE ESSENTIAL QUESTION**

13. Answers will vary, but students should demonstrate that they recognize many other environmental characteristics are affected by human activities.

Answer Key for INDEPENDENT Inquiry

ASK A QUESTION

1. Accept all reasonable answers.

Teacher Prompt Consider the ways humans use land and how that may affect the different kinds of plants that grow in a particular area.

FORM A PREDICTION

2. Accept all reasonable answers.

Teacher Prompt What types of events would have a negative impact on plants growing in an area, and who is responsible for causing those events?

MAKE A PLAN

3. Accept all reasonable answers.

Teacher Prompt How are your sites used by people?

Field Lab continued

4. Accept all reasonable answers. Students' data tables should include space for repeated sampling. A sample table is shown:

		Data and Observations			
		Trial #	Number of plant species found	Plant cover	Observations and notes
Type of land use	Lawn	1			
		2			
		3			
		4			
	Vacant lot	1			
		2			
		3			
		4			

ANALYZE THE RESULTS

11. Accept all reasonable answers.
Teacher Prompt Have you thought about calculating an average?

DRAW CONCLUSIONS

12. Accept all reasonable answers. Be sure that students' conclusions are consistent with the data they collected.

Connect TO THE ESSENTIAL QUESTION

13. Answers will vary, but students should demonstrate that they recognize that many other environmental characteristics are affected by human activities.

FIELD LAB GUIDED *Inquiry*

Field Investigation of Plant Quantity and Diversity

In this activity, you will choose two different outdoor sites to study. You will observe how much plant cover is associated with each site. You will also observe how many different species of plants are present at each site. You will use the data you collect to draw conclusions about what types of external influences may affect plant quantity and diversity.

PROCEDURE

ASK A QUESTION

① Within your group, consider the following types of areas: farm field, park, golf course, parking lot, nature reserve. Discuss the differences between these areas in terms of the variety of plant species that might be present and the total number of plants present. Develop a question to ask based on your discussion. You may either come up with your own question, or you may fill in the blank in the question below:

How do _____ impact the quantity and diversity of plants living in an area?

_____

_____

FORM A PREDICTION

② Within your group, discuss your thoughts on the answer to your question. Write your prediction below.

_____

_____

MAKE A PLAN

③ Find two different sites on a local map. Characterize each site with a general description (for example, lawn, golf course, park) and your estimate of the level of human impact (heavy, medium, light, none). Write down the sites you find.

_____

_____

_____

_____

OBJECTIVE

• Conduct field studies of plant quantity and diversity in two areas and use the results to draw conclusions about probable external influences.

MATERIALS

For each group
• field notebook
• map of local area
• plant identification key (optional)
• wire square, quadrat, 30 centimeters (cm) × 30 cm

For each student
• protective clothing suitable for field study

Field Lab continued

4 Read through the procedure you will follow. Work as a group to develop appropriate data tables to use during your field work and enter them in the space below. Obtain your teacher's approval of your data tables.

MAKE OBSERVATIONS

5 Travel to one of the sites you identified in Step 3. At the site, use the wire square to identify an area in which to look for plant species. One way to make sure you are not introducing bias into your sampling is to gently toss the wire square onto the area.

6 Count the number of different plant species within the wire square. Also determine whether each species is native or introduced. Record the information in your data table.

7 Count the number of individual plants of each species within the square. Record this information in your data table.

8 Estimate the proportion of plant cover and record. Do this by estimating how much of the square is covered by plants compared to how much is bare ground, cement, or asphalt.

9 Repeat Steps 5 to 8 until you have obtained a representative sample of the different kinds of plants in the site. You will know that you have a representative sample when you are no longer finding additional species each time you use the square. Use this random sampling process to obtain several samples at each site. This is important to ensure the maximum number of plant species is obtained for each site.

10 Repeat Steps 5 to 9 for your other site.

Field Lab continued

ANALYZE THE RESULTS

11 **Calculating Averages** You sampled each site repeatedly. You can pool the data by calculating the average number of plant species present and the average proportion of plant cover at each site. Make a table below to show your results for each of the two sites you studied.

DRAW CONCLUSIONS

12 **Evaluating Data** Compare the results you obtained for the two sites. Are they different? Do you see any relationship between the amount of human activity at a site and the quantity and diversity of plants present there? Explain.

_____

_____

_____

_____

Connect TO THE ESSENTIAL QUESTION

13 **Applying Concepts** Do you think that human impact affects other aspects of the natural environment in addition to any that you noted from this investigation? Explain.

_____

_____

_____

_____

FIELD LAB INDEPENDENT *Inquiry*

Field Investigation of Plant Quantity and Diversity

In this activity, you will choose two different outdoor sites to study. You will observe how much plant cover is associated with each site. You will also observe how many different species of plants are present at each site. You will use the data you collect to draw conclusions about what types of external influences may affect plant quantity and diversity.

PROCEDURE

ASK A QUESTION

1 Within your group, consider the following types of areas: farm field, park, golf course, parking lot, nature reserve. Discuss the differences between these areas in terms of the variety of plant species that might be present and the total number of plants present. Develop a question to ask based on your discussion.

_____

_____

FORM A PREDICTION

2 Within your group, discuss your thoughts on the answer to your question. Write your prediction below.

_____

_____

MAKE A PLAN

3 Find two different sites on a local map. Characterize each site with a general description (for example, lawn, golf course, park) and your estimate of the level of human impact (heavy, medium, light, none). Write down the sites you find.

_____

_____

_____

_____

OBJECTIVE
• Conduct field studies of plant quantity and diversity in two areas and use the results to draw conclusions about probable external influences.

MATERIALS
For each group
• field notebook
• map of local area
• plant identification key (optional)
• wire square quadrat, 30 centimeters (cm) × 30 (cm)

ScienceFusion
Module D Lab Manual

147

Unit 2, Lesson 5
Human Activity and Ecosystems

Original content Copyright © by Holt McDougal. Alterations to the original content are the responsibility of the instructor.

Field Lab continued

4 Read through the procedure you will follow. Work as a group to develop appropriate data tables to use during your field work and enter them in the space below. Obtain your teacher's approval of your data tables.

MAKE OBSERVATIONS

5 Travel to one of the sites you identified in Step 3. At the site, use the wire square to identify an area in which to look for plant species. One way to make sure you are not introducing bias into your sampling is to gently toss the wire square onto the area.

6 Count the number of different plant species within the wire square. Also determine whether each species is native or introduced. Record the information in your data table.

7 Count the number of individual plants of each species within the square. Record this information in your data table.

8 Estimate the proportion of plant cover and record. Do this by estimating how much of the square is covered by plants compared to how much is bare ground, cement, or asphalt.

9 Repeat Steps 5 to 8 until you have obtained a representative sample of the different kinds of plants in the site. You will know that you have a representative sample when you are no longer finding additional species each time you use the square. Use this random sampling process to obtain several samples at each site. This is important to ensure the maximum number of plant species is obtained for each site.

10 Repeat Steps 5 to 9 for your other site.

Field Lab continued

ANALYZE THE RESULTS

⑪ **Analyzing Data** You sampled each site repeatedly. Work with the other members of your group to decide how to analyze these numbers. Make a summary table below to show your results for each of the two sites you studied.

DRAW CONCLUSIONS

⑫ **Evaluating Data** Compare the results you obtained for the two sites. Are they different? Do you see any relationship between the amount of human activity at a site and the quantity and diversity of plants present there? Explain.

_____

_____

_____

_____

Connect TO THE ESSENTIAL QUESTION

⑬ **Applying Concepts** Do you think that human impact affects other aspects of the natural environment in addition to any that you noted from this investigation? Explain.

_____

_____

_____

_____

QUICK LAB DIRECTED *Inquiry*

How Water Forms on Earth's Surface GENERAL

👥 Small groups

🕐 20 minutes

LAB RATINGS

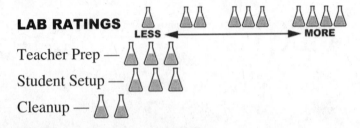

LESS ◀————————▶ MORE

Teacher Prep —

Student Setup —

Cleanup —

MATERIALS

For each group
- funnel
- ice
- jar, glass (400 mL capacity) with metal lid
- water, hot

For each student
- lab apron
- safety goggles

My Notes

_____

_____

_____

_____

_____

SAFETY INFORMATION

Remind students to review all safety cautions and icons before beginning this lab. Students should not handle hot water. They should wear goggles at all times during this activity and stand away as you pour hot water into their group's jar. Students should not touch the jar until you determine that it has reached a safe handling temperature.

TEACHER NOTES

In this activity, students will set up a model in a glass jar to observe how water vapor condenses and forms rain as it cools in Earth's atmosphere. Jars are used because of their heat resistance. You will pour hot water through a funnel into each group's jar and place a lid over the top of the bottle. Students will then add 2–3 ice cubes on top of the lid and observe changes taking place on the interior of the bottle.

This activity models the water cycle. Water evaporates from the Earth's surface, rises through the atmosphere, cools, and condenses. The concept of the water cycle provides a starting point for the discussion of this activity.

To prepare for this activity, it works best to heat water to boiling earlier in the day and store the heated water in a large thermos. You will need enough hot water to provide about 50 mL for each group. To avoid having students handling this hot water, have them set up their jars so that you can come around and dispense hot water for them. Be sure students stand away as you pour water from the thermos into their jar and then place the lid containing ice cubes over top. Caution them not to touch their bottle until the water has cooled back to a safe handling temperature.

Tip This activity helps students practice their observation skills.

Student Tip The water added to the bottle is hot, so be careful not to touch the jar after the water is added.

Skills Focus Making Observations, Interpreting Models

Quick Lab continued

MODIFICATION FOR GUIDED *Inquiry*

Provide students with the following challenge: With the materials provided, construct a situation in which you can observe how water vapor condenses and forms liquid water. Ask students to describe how the situation models the formation of rain as it cools in Earth's atmosphere.

Answer Key

PROCEDURE

3. Sample answer: Droplets of water form on the inside of the jar and run down the interior sides.

4. Sample answer: The hot water evaporates and increases the amount of water vapor in the air inside the jar. When the water vapor cools, it condenses in small drops on the interior sides of the jar.

5. Sample answer: The jar is a closed system similar to Earth. The jar also shows some of the changes in the state of water during the water cycle. It shows how water evaporates to move into the atmosphere and then later condenses to return back to Earth's surface.

6. Sample answer: The jar does not represent all of the complexities of Earth's atmosphere (such as global wind systems), nor does it have an outside heat source such as the sun.

7. Sample answer: Rain provides moisture for plant life. The water cycle also naturally cleans and recycles the water on Earth.

QUICK LAB DIRECTED *Inquiry*

How Water Forms on Earth's Surface

In this activity, your group will set up a model of the water cycle in a glass jar and observe how water vapor condenses and becomes rain as it cools in Earth's atmosphere. With the teacher's assistance, you will pour hot water through a funnel into the jar. Then you will add a lid to the top of the jar to trap the water vapor, and place ice cubes on the lid. You will need to observe the interior of the jar.

PROCEDURE

❶ Place the funnel in the bottle. Your teacher will add hot water to the container through the funnel. Once the water has been added, do not touch the container as it will be very hot.

❷ Remove the funnel and place an inverted metal lid on top of the bottle. The lid needs to be arranged so that vapor from the hot water cannot escape. Place several ice cubes on the inverted lid.

❸ Observe the interior of the bottle. Record your observations.

_____

_____

_____

❹ Explain why small drops of water collect on the inside surfaces of the bottle.

_____

_____

_____

❺ How does this model represent a process that occurs in Earth's atmosphere?

_____

_____

_____

OBJECTIVES

• Model the formation of rain in Earth's atmosphere.

• Explain the importance of rain for survival on Earth.

MATERIALS

For each group of students

• funnel

• ice

• jar, glass (400 mL capacity), with lid

• water, hot

For each student

• lab apron

• safety goggles

Quick Lab continued

6 Give at least one example of how this model does not represent the process you discussed in Question 5.

_____

_____

_____

_____

7 Explain two reasons why rain is important to life on Earth.

_____

_____

_____

_____

QUICK LAB DIRECTED Inquiry

Temperature Variations
on Earth GENERAL

👥 Small groups
🕐 20 minutes

LAB RATINGS

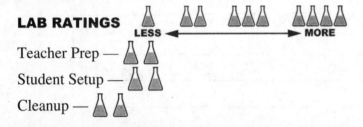

LESS ⟵——————⟶ MORE

Teacher Prep —

Student Setup —

Cleanup —

MATERIALS

For each group
• can, metal, large
• lamp
• stopwatch
• tape, masking
• thermometers, alcohol (2)

For each student
• safety goggles

SAFETY INFORMATION

Remind students to review all safety cautions and icons before beginning this lab. Students should use caution when working with the lamp and should never touch it when it is hot. Instruct students to wear heat-resistant gloves as they rotate the can.

TEACHER NOTES

In this activity, students will use a metal can as a model of the Earth. Students will tape two thermometers on opposite sides of the can. Using a heat source, students will model the Earth in two different ways. The first time, they will keep one thermometer facing the heat source and the other thermometer facing away from the heat source. The second time, they will slowly spin the model (approximately 1 spin for every 10 seconds). Students will keep track of the temperatures and compare the two approaches.

Tip This activity helps students practice measurement skills.

Student Tip The lamp is used as a heat source.

Skills Focus Making Measurements

My Notes

_____

_____

_____

_____

_____

MODIFICATION FOR GUIDED Inquiry

Provide students with the following challenge: With the materials provided, construct a situation in which you can observe how the Earth receives heat from the sun.

Answer Key for DIRECTED Inquiry

PROCEDURE

1. Accept all reasonable answers.

3. Sample answer: I think the thermometer near the lamp will increase in temperature, while the second thermometer will not change in temperature.

4. Sample data:

PART I

Thermometer	Initial temperature (^{0}C)	Final temperature (^{0}C)
A	23	23
B	26	43

5. Accept all reasonable answers.

7. Sample answer: I think the thermometers will both increase equally in temperature after five minutes.

8. Sample data:

PART II–ROTATING THE CAN

Thermometer	Initial temperature (^{0}C)	Final temperature (^{0}C)
A	23	37
B	23	37

9. Accept all reasonable answers. Students should observe a significant difference in temperature between the two thermometers.

10. Accept all reasonable answers. Students should observe a much smaller difference in temperature between the two thermometers and possibly no temperature difference at all.

11. Sample answer: Only one thermometer was near the lamp while the second thermometer was facing away from the lamp. Thus, one thermometer received a great deal of heat while the second thermometer received no direct heat.

12. Sample answer: Because the can was rotating at a fairly constant pace, each thermometer received an equal amount of heat from the lamp. This caused both thermometers to have a fairly equal increase in temperature.

13. Sample answer: Because the Earth rotates slowly over a 24–hour period, each side receives a fairly equal amount of heat from the sun.

14. Sample answer: If the Earth stopped rotating only one side would receive heat. This side would become incredibly hot while the opposite side of the Earth would remain cold.

Name _____ Class _____ Date _____

QUICK LAB DIRECTED Inquiry

Temperature Variations on Earth

In this activity, your group will use a metal can as a model of the Earth. You will begin by taping two thermometers on opposite sides of the can. Using a heat source, your group will model the Earth in two different ways. The first time, you will keep one thermometer facing the heat source and the other thermometer facing away from the heat source. The second time, you will slowly spin the model (approximately 1 spin for every 10 seconds). Your group will need to keep track of the temperatures and compare the two approaches.

PROCEDURE

1 Tape the two thermometers to opposite sides of the large metal can. Record the initial temperature of each thermometer.

_____

_____

2 Place the can about 20 centimeters (cm) away from the lamp. One thermometer should be facing the lamp, and the other should be facing away from the lamp. Label one thermometer "A" and the other "B."

3 Turn on the lamp. Predict what you think the final temperature of both thermometers will be after five minutes.

_____

_____

4 After 5 minutes (min), record the final temperatures of both thermometers and turn off the lamp.

_____

_____

5 Allow several minutes for the can and the thermometers to return to the initial temperatures you recorded before the first trial. Record the initial temperatures of both thermometers.

_____

_____

6 Turn on the lamp and use heat-resistant gloves to rotate the can slowly so that it makes 1 complete rotation every 10 seconds. Take turns rotating the can because you will need to continue rotating the can for 5 min.

OBJECTIVE

- Observe how temperatures vary on Earth as a result of its rotating motion.

MATERIALS

For each group
- can, metal, large
- lamp
- stopwatch
- tape, masking
- thermometers, alcohol (2)

For each student
- safety goggles

Quick Lab continued

7 Predict what you think the final temperature of both thermometers will be after 5 min.

_____

8 After 5 minutes of rotation, record the final temperature of both thermometers and turn off the lamp.

_____

9 What was the difference between the initial temperature and final temperature for each thermometer in the first trial?

_____

10 What was the difference between the initial temperature and final temperature for each thermometer in the second trial?

_____

11 Explain your observations from the first trial.

_____

_____

12 Explain your observations from the second trial.

_____

_____

13 Explain how the second trial models how Earth is heated by the sun.

_____

_____

_____

14 Predict what would happen if Earth stopped rotating.

_____

_____

_____

_____

EXPLORATION LAB GUIDED Inquiry AND INDEPENDENT Inquiry

Modeling the Greenhouse Effect GENERAL

👥 Small groups
🕐 45 minutes

LAB RATINGS

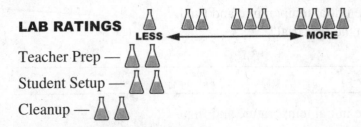

LESS ◄─────────► MORE

Teacher Prep —

Student Setup —

Cleanup —

MATERIALS

For each group of students

• box, cardboard (2)
• lamp
• plastic wrap
• soil, potting
• tape, masking
• thermometers, alcohol (2)

My Notes

_____

_____

_____

_____

_____

SAFETY INFORMATION

Remind students to review all safety cautions and icons before beginning this lab. Be sure that students wear safety goggles, gloves, and a lab apron when using the potting soil to construct their models. Have students wash and dry their hands after completing the inquiry.

TEACHER NOTES

Students will design and build a model of the greenhouse effect on Earth. The plastic wrap that students will use in the model represents the greenhouse gases that help trap the heat from Earth. Students can either use a heat lamp or take their models outside to use in the sun if weather permits. Students will use their model to investigate how changing one variable within the model affects its ability to trap energy coming in from the lamp or the sun. Some variables to test include the color of the plastic wrap, the number of layers of plastic wrap, and the length of time the model is exposed to the heat lamp.

In the Guided Inquiry, students will be provided the problem and materials list in order to design the investigation. For the independent inquiry, students will be provided the problem, but will need to generate their own materials list to carry out the designed investigation.

Tip Students may require prompting to use the plastic wrap as a greenhouse gas. Remind students that the Earth's atmosphere is transparent, so the material they use to signify greenhouse gases also needs to be transparent.

Student Tip When brainstorming a design, think about what needs to be modeled.

Skills Focus Devising Procedures, Making Models

MODIFICATION FOR DIRECTED Inquiry

Provide students with a written procedure describing how to set up the model and collect data.

Answer Key for GUIDED Inquiry

DEVELOP A PLAN

2. Sample Answer: Cardboard box = the Earth and atmosphere. Lamp = the sun. Plastic wrap = greenhouse gases. Potting soil = the Earth's surface.

3. Accept all reasonable answers. A possible variable is the amount of potting soil.

FORM A HYPOTHESIS

4. Accept all reasonable answers.

TEST THE HYPOTHESIS

5. Sample Answer:

   a. Fill one cardboard box one-third of the way with potting soil and the second cardboard box one-half of the way with potting soil.

   b. Stand a thermometer upright in the potting soil of each box.

   c. Cover both boxes with one layer of plastic wrap. Place the boxes under a heat lamp (or outside, if it is sunny and warm).

   d. Observe and record temperatures inside both boxes over a 20-minute time span.

TEMPERATURE (^{0}C)

Time	Box $\frac{1}{3}$ full	Box $\frac{1}{2}$ full
0 minutes	19	19
10 minutes	20.5	19.75
20 minutes	21.5	20.5

ANALYZE THE RESULTS

6. Accept all reasonable answers.

7. Accept all reasonable answers.

DRAW CONCLUSIONS

8. Accept all reasonable answers.

9. Sample answer: Greenhouse gases. The plastic wrap is like a greenhouse gas because it slows the amount of heat that escapes the model. The plastic wrap is different from a greenhouse gas in that it is solid, not gaseous.

Exploration Lab continued

Connect TO THE ESSENTIAL QUESTION

10. Sample answer: In a moderate amount, greenhouse gases are helpful to the survival of life on Earth. Greenhouse gases trap energy from the sun, keeping Earth at a controlled, favorable temperature. This temperate climate allows water to be found in all three states: solid, liquid, and gas.

Answer Key for INDEPENDENT Inquiry

DEVELOP A PLAN

2. Sample answer: Cardboard box = the Earth and atmosphere. Lamp = the sun. Plastic wrap = greenhouse gases. Potting soil = the Earth's surface.

3. Accept all reasonable answers. A possible variable would be the amount of amount of plastic wrap used.

FORM A HYPOTHESIS

4. Accept all reasonable answers. A possible hypothesis is that adding more layers of plastic wrap will increase the difference between the initial and final temperatures because more layers of plastic will trap more heat.

TEST THE HYPOTHESIS

5. Sample Answer:

   a. Wrap one layer of plastic over the top of the first cardboard box and three layers of plastic wrap over the top of the second cardboard box.

   b. Stand a thermometer upright in the potting soil of each box.

   c. Cover one box with one layer of plastic wrap. Cover the second box with four layers of plastic wrap. Place the boxes under a heat lamp (or outside, if it is sunny and warm).

   d. Observe and record temperatures inside both boxes over a 20-minute time span.

ANALYZE THE RESULTS

6. Accept all reasonable answers.

7. Accept all reasonable answers.

DRAW CONCLUSIONS

8. Accept all reasonable answers.

9. Sample answer: Greenhouse gases. The plastic wrap is like a greenhouse gas because it slows the amount of heat that escapes the model. The plastic wrap is different from a greenhouse gas in that it is solid, not gaseous.

Connect TO THE ESSENTIAL QUESTION

10. Sample answer: In a moderate amount, greenhouse gases are helpful to the survival of life on Earth. Greenhouse gases trap energy from the sun, keeping Earth at a controlled, favorable temperature. This temperate climate allows water to be found in all three states: solid, liquid, and gas.

EXPLORATION LAB GUIDED Inquiry

Modeling the Greenhouse Effect

In this lab, you will design and construct a model that represents the greenhouse effect on Earth. You will then use your model to investigate how changing one variable in your model affects the model's ability to trap energy coming in to the model.

PROCEDURE

ASK A QUESTION

❶ Greenhouse gases play an important role in maintaining temperatures on Earth's surface that are favorable for life. These gases are found in Earth's atmosphere and trap energy from the sun so it cannot leave the atmosphere once it has entered. In this lab, you will be investigating the question, "How can the greenhouse effect be modeled?"

DEVELOP A PLAN

❷ Work with the members of your group to find a way to use the materials provided to make a model of the greenhouse effect. For each material, explain what it will represent in your model: cardboard box, lamp, plastic wrap, potting soil.

_____

_____

_____

_____

❸ From the list of materials in Step 2, choose one as a variable for your group to test. You will be investigating to see how this variable affects the trapping of energy in your model.

_____

_____

FORM A HYPOTHESIS

❹ Using the variable that your group identified in Step 3, write a hypothesis for your investigation.

_____

_____

OBJECTIVES

• Create a model of the greenhouse effect on Earth.

• Describe how the greenhouse effect in Earth's atmosphere helps sustain life on Earth.

MATERIALS

For each group of students
• box, cardboard (2)
• lamp
• plastic wrap
• soil, potting
• tape, masking
• thermometers, alcohol (2)

For each student
• lab apron
• safety goggles

Exploration Lab continued

TEST THE HYPOTHESIS

5 Design a plan for testing your hypothesis. Record your plan in the space below. Make sure to describe how you will collect and organize your data. Once you have developed a plan, ask for your teacher's approval before continuing.

_____

_____

_____

_____

_____

ANALYZE THE RESULTS

6 **Analyzing Data** What is the difference between the initial and final temperatures of each thermometer?

_____

_____

_____

7 **Interpreting Data** Write a sentence or two that explains the difference (if any) between the initial and final temperatures of each thermometer.

_____

_____

_____

DRAW CONCLUSIONS

8 **Evaluating Hypotheses** Review your hypothesis from Step 3. Do your data support your hypothesis? If not, revise your hypothesis below.

_____

_____

_____

_____

Exploration Lab continued

9 **Evaluating Models** In the model, the plastic wrap represents
_____, a part of Earth's atmosphere. Explain how
the plastic wrap accurately represents this part and how the plastic wrap
does not accurately represent this part.

_____

_____

_____

_____

Connect **TO THE ESSENTIAL QUESTION**

10 **Explaining Concepts** Explain how the unique properties of Earth allow
life to exist.

_____

_____

_____

_____

EXPLORATION LAB INDEPENDENT *Inquiry*

Modeling the Greenhouse Effect

In this lab, you will design and construct a model that represents the greenhouse effect on Earth. You will then use your model to investigate how changing one variable in your model affects the model's ability to trap energy coming in to the model.

PROCEDURE

ASK A QUESTION

❶ Greenhouse gases play an important role in maintaining temperatures on Earth's surface that are favorable for life. These gases are found in Earth's atmosphere and trap energy from the sun so it cannot leave the atmosphere once it has entered. In this lab, you will be investigating the question, "How can the greenhouse effect be modeled?"

DEVELOP A PLAN

❷ Develop a list of materials that you will need to construct your model. Consider the following parts of the Earth that will need to be represented: Earth's surface, the sun, greenhouse gases, the atmosphere.

_____

_____

_____

❸ From the list of materials in Step 2, choose one as a variable for your group to test. You will be investigating to see how this variable affects the trapping of energy in your model.

_____

_____

FORM A HYPOTHESIS

❹ Using the variable that your group identified in Step 3, write a hypothesis for your investigation.

_____

_____

OBJECTIVES

- Create a model of the greenhouse effect on Earth.
- Describe how the greenhouse effect in Earth's atmosphere helps sustain life on Earth.

MATERIALS

For each group
- box, cardboard (2)
- lamp
- plastic wrap
- soil, potting
- tape, masking
- thermometers, alcohol (2)

For each student
- lab apron
- safety goggles

Exploration Lab continued

TEST THE HYPOTHESIS

❺ Design a plan for testing your hypothesis. Record your plan in the space below. Make sure to describe how you will collect and organize your data. Once you have developed a plan, ask for your teacher's approval before continuing.

_____

_____

_____

_____

_____

ANALYZE THE RESULTS

❻ **Analyzing Data** What is the difference between the initial and final temperatures of each thermometer?

_____

_____

_____

❼ **Interpreting Data** Write a sentence or two that explains the difference (if any) between the initial and final temperatures of each thermometer.

_____

_____

_____

_____

DRAW CONCLUSIONS

❽ **Evaluating Hypotheses** Review your hypothesis from Step 3. Do your data support your hypothesis? If not, revise your hypothesis below.

_____

_____

_____

Exploration Lab continued

9 **Evaluating Models** In the model, the plastic wrap represents _____, a part of Earth's atmosphere. Explain how the plastic wrap accurately represents this part and how the plastic wrap does not accurately represent this part.

_____

_____

_____

_____

Connect **TO THE ESSENTIAL QUESTION**

10 **Explaining Concepts** Explain how the unique properties of Earth allow life to exist.

_____

_____

_____

_____

QUICK LAB DIRECTED *Inquiry*

Renewable or Not? GENERAL

👥 Small groups
🕐 15 minutes

LAB RATINGS

LESS ⟵⟶ MORE

Teacher Prep —

Student Setup —

Cleanup —

MATERIALS

For each group
• paper cup
• pencil
• sink or basin
• water
  (at least 2 cups)
For each student
• lab apron
• safety goggles

SAFETY INFORMATION

Remind students to review all safety cautions and icons before beginning this lab. Clean up any spills immediately to avoid slipping.

TEACHER NOTES

In this activity, students will model the rate of resource formation or replacement and the rate of resource use. Students will see how these factors combine to determine whether a resource is renewable or nonrenewable.

Tip This activity may help students better understand the difference between renewable and nonrenewable resources.

Skills Focus Making Models, Drawing Conclusions

My Notes

_____

_____

_____

_____

_____

MODIFICATION FOR GUIDED *Inquiry*

Have students modify this investigation so that it models a renewable resource. How can they use water to demonstrate a renewable resource? Students should write a procedure that describes the steps they will take, including all the materials they will use. Approve all reasonable procedures, and allow students to carry out their experiments.

MODIFICATION FOR INDEPENDENT *Inquiry*

Energy resources are an important issue in today's world. Have students research some examples of renewable and nonrenewable energy resources. Students should compare the environmental and financial costs and benefits of each type of resource. They should present their conclusions in a lab report.

Answer Key

3. Sample answer: the water

4. Sample answer: The water pouring into the cup is resource formation, and the water dripping out through the holes is resource consumption.

5. Sample answer: This model represents a nonrenewable resource because there is no new resource being formed to replace the resource that is consumed.

6. Sample answer: A resource is renewable if it can be replaced at the same rate as it is used. A resource is nonrenewable if it cannot be replaced.

QUICK LAB DIRECTED *Inquiry*

Renewable or Not?

In this lab, you will use a model to observe rates of resource formation or replacement and the rate of resource use. You will observe how these factors relate to whether a resource is renewable or nonrenewable.

PROCEDURE

1 Using the **pencil,** carefully punch three holes in the bottom of the **cup.** Make a pencil mark on the inside of the cup about 2 cm from the bottom.

2 Hold the cup over a **basin** or **sink.** Pour **water** into the cup to the level of the pencil mark.

3 Which part of this model represents a resource?

_____

_____

_____

_____

4 Which part of the model represents resource formation? Resource consumption?

_____

_____

_____

_____

_____

OBJECTIVE
• Compare renewable and nonrenewable resources using a model.

MATERIALS
For each group
• paper cup
• pencil
• sink or basin
• water
  (at least 2 cups)
For each group
• lab apron
• safety goggles

Quick Lab continued

❺ Is the resource in the model renewable or nonrenewable? Explain.

_____

_____

_____

_____

❻ What makes a resource renewable or nonrenewable?

_____

_____

_____

_____

_____

QUICK LAB DIRECTED Inquiry

Production Impacts GENERAL

👥 Small groups
🕐 15 minutes

MATERIALS
For each group
- finished product
- raw material

LAB RATINGS

LESS ⬅————➡ MORE

Teacher Prep —

Student Setup —

Cleanup —

My Notes

_____
_____
_____
_____
_____

SAFETY INFORMATION

Remind students to review all safety cautions and icons before beginning this lab. Safety concerns will vary depending on the materials given to students. Possible dangers include exposure to sharp objects or allergens.

TEACHER NOTES

In this activity, students will use research resources you designate to identify the origins of raw materials and the ways in which these materials are processed to create a finished product. Examples of pairs of raw material and finished product include ore and a student's metal-framed chair, wood and a pencil, sand and a glass bottle, and raw cotton and a T-shirt. You may wish to give students photographs or drawings of one or more of the materials rather than the actual objects.

Tip This activity may help students understand that the production of many common items impacts Earth on a number of levels.

Student Tip For each step, think about the resources consumed and the waste generated to complete each task involved.

Skills Focus Making Inferences, Applying Concepts

MODIFICATION FOR GUIDED Inquiry

Provide students with samples of a raw material and its finished product. Ask students to research and present how the production and consumption of the finished product impacts the environment on a variety of levels.

Answer Key

1. Answers will vary.
2. Answers will vary.
3. Answers will vary.
4. Answers will vary.
5. Answers will vary.

QUICK LAB DIRECTED *Inquiry*

Production Impacts

In this lab, you will explain how a product is made from a raw
material and examine the environmental impacts of that process.

PROCEDURE

1 Look at your raw material. Is it a renewable resource? How do
people get this material from Earth?

_____

_____

_____

_____

_____

2 What kinds of resources are used to get the raw material? How does the use
of those resources impact Earth's environment?

_____

_____

_____

_____

_____

_____

3 Look at your final product. How is it created from your raw material?

_____

_____

_____

_____

_____

_____

OBJECTIVE
• Explain how the production of common items impacts Earth in a variety of ways.
MATERIALS
For each group
• finished product
• raw material

Quick Lab continued

4 What kinds of resources are used to create and deliver the final product? How does the use of those resources impact Earth's environment?

_____

_____

_____

_____

_____

5 How long does the finished product last? What happens to the final product when the consumer is finished with it? How does this impact Earth's environment?

_____

_____

_____

_____

_____

_____

FIELD LAB DIRECTED Inquiry **AND** GUIDED Inquiry

Natural Resources Used at Lunch GENERAL

MATERIALS

For each group
- balance or scale
- lunch waste
- paper towels

For each student
- calculator
- gloves
- lab apron
- mask, disposable filter
- safety goggles

👥 Small groups
🕐 45 minutes

LAB RATINGS

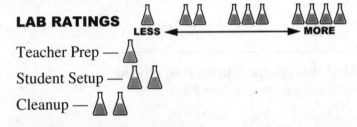

LESS ◄─────────► MORE

Teacher Prep —

Student Setup —

Cleanup —

SAFETY INFORMATION

Remind students to review all safety cautions and icons before beginning this lab. Warn students that the trash may contain bacteria or allergens, and they should wash their hands at the end of the lab. Warn students to handle trash carefully; some waste may have sharp edges.

TEACHER NOTES

In this activity, students will collect and analyze the trash they generated during their lunch period in order to determine what natural resources were consumed. You will need to tell your students the total number of people in your school, including faculty, staff, and students. For easy cleanup, you may choose to perform this activity in the school cafeteria rather than in the classroom. If the activity takes place in the classroom, be sure to sanitize all surfaces and materials used.

Tip This lab may help students understand how their product consumption impacts the environment.

Student Tip Plastic is made from petroleum. Polystyrene is a type of plastic.

Skills Focus Collecting Evidence, Classifying Samples

My Notes

_____

_____

_____

_____

_____

MODIFICATION FOR INDEPENDENT Inquiry

Have the class brainstorm a list of natural resources they commonly use. Ask students to select one natural resource and observe and record their family's consumption of that resource over a brief period of time (e.g., an hour or an evening). Encourage them to think of ways to quantify their results, such as recording the amount of or length of time the resource was used. Examples of data gathered could be the amount of time each light was left on, the gallons of gas consumed, and the number of paper towels used. Ask students to review their findings with their families and make a list of ways to reduce their consumption of natural resources.

Field Lab continued

Answer Key for DIRECTED Inquiry

FORM A HYPOTHESIS

2. Sample answer: I think they will be similar because plastic and paper are probably used more but have less mass. Metal and glass are heavier but are less commonly used.

TEST THE HYPOTHESIS

5. Answers will vary.

6. Answers will vary.

7. Answers will vary.

ANALYZE THE RESULTS

8. Sample answer: The results all seem to be pretty similar. Most people used plastic bags to hold their food and paper cartons or boxes to hold their drinks, so the masses were similar among the groups. Some groups had lower paper masses if they packed their lunches in lunchboxes or bought their lunch in the cafeteria.

9. Answers will vary.

DRAW CONCLUSIONS

10. Answers will vary.

Connect TO THE ESSENTIAL QUESTION

11. Sample answer: I think the school should try to encourage students to use reusable packages for their lunches because plastic is not biodegradable and it comes from oil, which is a non-renewable resource. They should also require students to recycle as much of their waste as possible so that we can reuse those natural resources.

Answer Key for GUIDED Inquiry

FORM A PREDICTION

2. Sample answer: bags (paper, plastic), juice and milk cartons (paper), straws (plastic), wrappers (paper, plastic, metal), bottles (plastic, glass), napkins (paper)

DEVELOP A PLAN

3. Sample answer: We will go through the trash and put it into one of the following categories: paper/wood, plastic, metal, and glass.

4. Sample answer: We will use a scale to measure the mass of all the waste in each category. This is a good method because it gives a better idea of the actual amount of each resource used. We might have a large number of small or lightweight things like paper and one heavy thing like a glass bottle. Counting the items would make it seem like there was a lot more plastic used than glass, but that might not be true.

Field Lab continued

5. Sample answer: We can calculate what percentage of the total mass is made up of the mass of each type of waste.

6. Sample answer: We can divide the mass of each type of waste by the number of students in the group.

7. Sample answer: We will sort all of the trash into the four categories of natural resources (paper, plastic, metal, and glass) and then use a scale to measure the mass of each type of waste. We will also add up the masses of the different types of waste to determine the total mass of all the waste. To find what percentage of waste is made of each type of natural resource, we will divide each type's mass by the total waste's mass and multiply that number by 100. To figure out the average waste generated by each student, we will divide the mass of each type of waste by the number of students in the group.

ANALYZE THE RESULTS

8. Sample answer: The results all seem to be pretty similar. Most people used plastic bags to hold their food and paper cartons or boxes to hold their drinks, so the masses were similar among the groups. Some groups had lower paper masses if they packed their lunches in lunchboxes or bought their lunch in the cafeteria.

9. Answers will vary.

DRAW CONCLUSIONS

10. Answers will vary.

Connect TO THE ESSENTIAL QUESTION

11. Sample answer: I think the school should try to encourage students to use reusable packages for their lunches because plastic comes from petroleum, which is a non-renewable resource. Plastic also does not biodegrade. They should also require students to recycle as much of their waste as possible so that we can reuse those natural resources.

Natural Resources Used at Lunch

In this lab, you will analyze the trash produced during your lunch
period to determine what natural resources were consumed. You
will then recommend steps your school can take to reduce its use of
natural resources.

PROCEDURE

ASK A QUESTION

1 In this lab, you will analyze the trash you collect at lunch to
answer the following question: What percentage of the materials
left over after lunch come from each of the following categories:
paper and wood products, plastic, metal, and glass?

FORM A HYPOTHESIS

2 Write a hypothesis that is a possible answer to the question
above. Explain your reasoning.

_____

_____

_____

_____

_____

_____

_____

TEST THE HYPOTHESIS

3 Collect all of your **lunch waste** on the day of the lab activity or the day
before the lab activity, depending on whether your class meets before or
after lunch. Include all disposable waste, and be sure to empty out any
unfinished food or beverages.

4 Cover a flat surface with **paper towels**, and spread your group's lunch waste
on the surface. Organize the waste according to whether it is made from
paper/wood, plastic, metal, or glass.

OBJECTIVES

- Identify and
measure the natural
resources contained
in the waste from a
meal.
- Suggest ways to
minimize your
school's impact on
the environment.

MATERIALS

For each group
- balance or scale
- lunch waste
- paper towels

For each student
- calculator
- gloves
- lab apron
- mask, disposable
filter
- safety goggles

ScienceFusion
Module D Lab Manual

177

Unit 3, Lesson 2
Natural Resources

Original content Copyright © by Holt McDougal. Alterations to the original content are the responsibility of the instructor.

Field Lab continued

5 Use a **balance or scale** to measure the mass of the waste in each category. Calculate the total mass of all the waste. Record your data in the table below.

6 Use your data and a **calculator** to calculate the average mass of each type of waste produced per student. Record your data in the table below. Thoroughly wash your hands immediately after handling the lunch waste.

7 Calculate what percentage of the mass of the total waste is made up of each type of material. Record your data in the table.

Waste type	Mass (grams)	Average mass per student (grams)	Percentage of total mass
paper/wood			
plastic			
metal			
glass			

Total mass of all waste: _____

ANALYZE THE RESULTS

8 **Examining Data** Compare your group's data with the results from other groups in the class. How and why are the data similar or different?

_____

_____

_____

_____

_____

_____

_____

Field Lab continued

9 **Classifying Samples** What percentage of your group's waste came from renewable resources? What portion came from non-renewable resources?

_____

_____

_____

_____

_____

_____

DRAW CONCLUSIONS

10 **Making Predictions** Determine what mass of each type of waste is generated by your school at lunch each day. You may need to ask your teacher how many students, teachers, and staff members there are at your school.

_____

_____

_____

_____

_____

Connect TO THE ESSENTIAL QUESTION

11 **Applying Concepts** Describe at least two things you would recommend that your school do to minimize its impact on the environment. Base your recommendations on the data you have collected during this activity and on what you know about the material resources you have been studying.

_____

_____

_____

_____

_____

_____

_____

FIELD LAB GUIDED Inquiry

Natural Resources Used at Lunch

In this lab, you will analyze the trash produced during your lunch period to determine what natural resources were consumed. You will then recommend steps your school can take to reduce its use of natural resources.

PROCEDURE

MAKE OBSERVATIONS

❶ Collect all of your **lunch waste** on the day of the lab activity or the day before the lab activity, depending on whether your class meets before or after lunch. Include all disposable waste, and be sure to empty out any unfinished food or beverages.

FORM A PREDICTION

❷ With your group, brainstorm some of the types of trash usually produced during lunch. Make a list of some examples and the natural resource(s) from which they are made.

_____

_____

_____

_____

_____

DEVELOP A PLAN

❸ Now that you have a list of some of the natural resources used during lunch, how will you sort and classify the **lunch waste** you collected? Thoroughly wash your hands after handling and sorting lunch waste.

_____

_____

_____

OBJECTIVES

• Identify and measure the natural resources contained in the waste from a meal.

• Suggest ways to minimize your school's impact on the environment.

MATERIALS

For each group
• balance or scale
• lunch waste
• paper towels

For each student
• calculator
• gloves
• lab apron
• mask, disposable filter
• safety googles

Field Lab continued

4 How will you measure the amount of each type of natural resource that was used? Justify your answer.

_____

_____

_____

_____

_____

5 How can you use your data to figure out what proportion of waste is made of each type of natural resource?

_____

_____

_____

_____

_____

6 How can you use your data to figure out the average student's contributions to each type of waste?

_____

_____

_____

_____

_____

7 Briefly describe your experimental plan. Include all the materials you will use and any calculations you will make.

_____

_____

_____

_____

_____

_____

_____

_____

_____

Field Lab continued

ANALYZE THE RESULTS

8 **Examining Data** Compare your group's data with the results from other groups in the class. How and why are the data similar or different?

_____

_____

_____

_____

9 **Classifying Samples** What portion of your group's waste came from renewable resources? What portion came from non-renewable resources?

_____

_____

_____

DRAW CONCLUSIONS

10 **Making Predictions** Determine how much of each type of waste is generated by your school at lunch each day. You may need to ask your teacher how many students, teachers, and staff members there are at your school.

_____

_____

_____

_____

_____

Field Lab continued

Connect TO THE ESSENTIAL QUESTION

11 **Applying Concepts** Describe at least two things you would recommend that your school do to minimize its impact on the environment. Base your recommendations on the data you have collected during this activity and on what you know about the material resources you have been studying.

_____

_____

_____

_____

_____

_____

QUICK LAB GUIDED *Inquiry*

Modeling Nonrenewable Resources BASIC

👥 Student pairs

🕐 15 minutes

LAB RATINGS

LESS ◄——————► MORE

Teacher Prep —

Student Setup —

Cleanup —

MATERIALS

For each pair
- bag, paper lunch
- buttons (93 of one color and 7 of another color)

My Notes

_____

_____

_____

_____

_____

TEACHER NOTES

In this activity, students will make a model to show that nonrenewable resources are finite, while renewable resources can be replaced at the same rate they are used. Any small objects can be used in place of the buttons, as long as 93 of them are one color or style and 7 are a second color or style. Alternatively, you can have students use a hole punch to make small circles or use scissors to cut out 100 circles from paper. Color 7 of these one color and the other 93 a different color or write the letter *N* (for nonrenewable) on 93 of them and *R* (for renewable) on 7 of them. Ask students what percentage of 100 each color is. Explain that 93% of energy consumption in the United States comes from nonrenewable resources, while only 7% comes from renewable resources.

Tip This activity may help students better understand the finite nature of the most common and widely used energy sources. When students have completed the activity, you may wish to have them extend it by writing a science fiction story about a world without nonrenewable energy resources.

Student Tip What energy resources did you use today? Do you think that the sources of energy represented by these examples will always be available?

Skills Focus Drawing Conclusions, Making Models

MODIFICATION FOR INDEPENDENT *Inquiry*

Have students design an experiment in which they can model the finite nature of nonrenewable energy sources. Once you have approved their plans, have students carry out their experiment. Have volunteers share their procedure and results with the class. Encourage students to explain why they chose the materials they used and the procedure they followed.

Answer Key

1. 93 black buttons, 7 green buttons (if black and green buttons are used)

3. Students' tables should have three columns to record the trial number, the number of black buttons, and the number of green buttons. Each row represents a separate trial. An example is shown:

MODELING NONRENEWABLE RESOURCES

Trial number	Number of black buttons	Number of green buttons

7. The number of black buttons will vary but will be less than the amount originally used. All 7 green buttons will be in the bag.

8. The number of black buttons decreased, while the number of green buttons stayed the same.

9. The green buttons represented renewable resources. Placing them back in the bag showed that these resources are replenished at the same rate they are used. The black buttons represented nonrenewable resources. Once they are used, they cannot be replaced.

10. Sample answer: Nonrenewable resources will eventually run out because there is no way to replace them as quickly as they are being use.

QUICK LAB GUIDED *Inquiry*

Modeling Nonrenewable Resources

Most of the energy consumed in the United States comes from nonrenewable resources. In this activity, you will model what happens when a resource is consumed faster than it can be replaced.

PROCEDURE

OBJECTIVE
- Explain why some resources are nonrenewable.

MATERIALS
For each pair
- bag, paper lunch
- buttons (93 of one color and 7 of another color)

1 Ninety-three percent of the energy used in the United States comes from nonrenewable resources. How can you use the buttons provided by your teacher to represent both nonrenewable energy resources and renewable energy resources?

Teacher Prompt How many buttons do you need to represent the percentage of nonrenewable resources? How many buttons do you need to represent renewable resources?

_____

_____

2 Count out the buttons and put them in a paper bag.

3 Create a data table below to record the trial number, the number of buttons representing nonrenewable resources, and the number of buttons representing renewable resources. Add a row for each trial or for each time you will pull buttons out of the bag.

4 Without looking, take 10 buttons out of the bag. Set the nonrenewable buttons aside. Record the number of each type of button in your data table.

5 Put all renewable buttons back in the bag and shake the bag to mix the contents. Then, take out 10 more buttons. Continue building your data table by recording the results from this step.

6 Repeat Step 5 eight more times. Build on to your data table as before.

7 Place the remaining buttons in the bag onto your workspace. How many nonrenewable buttons are there? How many renewable buttons?

_____

Quick Lab continued

8 How did the number of nonrenewable buttons change from the beginning of the experiment to the end? How did the number of renewable buttons change?

_____

_____

9 Why did you set the nonrenewable buttons aside and place the renewable buttons back in the bag at each step?

_____

_____

_____

_____

10 Based on your experiment, what conclusions can you draw about nonrenewable resources?

_____

_____

QUICK LAB

Modeling Nuclear Fission GENERAL

👥 Large groups
⏱ 15 minutes

LAB RATINGS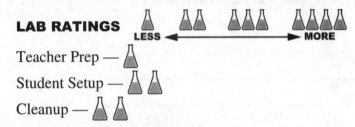

Teacher Prep —

Student Setup —

Cleanup —

MATERIALS

For each student
• balloon
• safety goggles
• toothpicks (2)

My Notes

_____

_____

_____

_____

_____

SAFETY INFORMATION

Remind students to review all safety cautions and icons before beginning this lab. Caution students to be careful when blowing up the balloons. They must not inhale the air from the balloon, as it may cause them to inhale the toothpick as well. Warn students that the toothpicks must be used only to pop a balloon. Tell students that they must hold the balloon as far away as possible from their faces when it is popped with a toothpick. Safety goggles must be worn to protect eyes in case any toothpicks fly toward the face.

TEACHER NOTES

In this activity, the class will work together to model nuclear fission. Explain that energy is released during nuclear fission reactions. Uranium-235 is a common nuclear fuel. When a free neutron strikes a uranium-235 atom, the atom splits into two smaller atoms. Two neutrons are also released in this process along with a large quantity of energy. The free neutrons strike other uranium-235 atoms, which starts a chain reaction.

To save some time, complete Step 1 for students. In Step 2, you will initiate the fission reaction by popping one student's balloon. That student will then use the toothpicks in his or her balloon to pop two more students' balloons. This process will go on until all balloons have been popped.

Tip This activity may help students better understand the chain reaction in nuclear fission. Ask volunteers to describe what happens in any chain reaction. You may also wish to have students model a chain reaction using dominoes.

Skills Focus Building Models, Explaining Processes

MODIFICATION FOR INDEPENDENT Inquiry

Have students come up with a plan to make a model of nuclear fission. Allow students to use any materials that are readily available in the classroom. Remind them that they need to show the free neutrons and the release of energy. After you have approved students' plans, have them carry out their plans. Have volunteers share their models and results with the class.

Answer Key

3. Sample answer: Yes, the balloon popped, which represents a release of energy.

4. Sample answer: Two toothpicks were released. These represent two neutrons from the uranium-235 atom.

6. Accept all reasonable answers. Students' diagrams should show the nature of a chain reaction (i.e., one neutron causes the release of two neutrons that cause the release of four more that cause the release of eight and then sixteen and so on.)

7. Sample answer: The reactions occur in a series or a chain with one reaction causing the next.

8. Sample answer: The energy would increase because more and more atoms are reacting.

9. Sample answer: If not controlled, the chain reaction would keep causing more and more atoms to react, and the amount of energy released could become too large to manage.

QUICK LAB GUIDED Inquiry

Modeling Nuclear Fission

In this activity, you will make a model to demonstrate a nuclear fission chain reaction. Nuclear power plants rely on the energy from fission reactions to generate electrical energy.

PROCEDURE

1 Carefully insert two toothpicks into an un-inflated balloon. Use care so as not to puncture the balloon. Blow up the balloon and tie off the end.

2 When everyone has a balloon ready, your teacher will initiate the fission reaction.

3 What represents the release of energy during this simulation of a nuclear chain reaction? Explain.

_____

_____

4 What else was released in the reaction? Explain what this represents in a nuclear fission reaction with uranium-235.

_____

_____

5 The student whose balloon was popped will now continue with the model by popping two more balloons. Keep going with your model until it is not possible to continue any longer.

6 On a separate sheet of paper, draw a flowchart or diagram to show what happened during the modeling exercise.

7 Why is this called a chain reaction?

_____

_____

OBJECTIVE

• Model a nuclear fission chain reaction.

MATERIALS

For each student
• balloon
• safety goggles
• toothpicks (2)

Quick Lab continued

8 Would you expect the amount of energy released during a nuclear chain reaction to increase, decrease, or stay constant? Explain.

_____

_____

9 Why would it be important to control a chain reaction in a nuclear power plant?

_____

_____

_____

QUICK LAB **INDEPENDENT** Inquiry

Design a Turbine GENERAL

👥 Small groups

🕐 30 minutes

LAB RATINGS

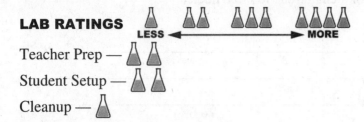

LESS ⟷ MORE

Teacher Prep —

Student Setup —

Cleanup —

SAFETY INFORMATION

Remind students to review all safety cautions and icons before beginning this lab. Students should use caution when working with the various materials, as some will have sharp edges. Remind students to clean up water spills immediately to reduce slipping hazards. Keep plenty of paper towels on hand for mopping up spills.

TEACHER NOTES

In this activity, students will build a model of a simple water turbine. Students will select which materials they will use from the list, provided, but they can make appropriate substitutions where allowable. Students should design their models without any instructions. After you approve each model, students will test their designs by pouring a set amount of water at a set rate over the turbine. Work with students to develop the volume of water and the rate at which they will pour it (as described in Procedure Step 3). In this way, students will be able to accurately compare results among groups. Finally, students should brainstorm ways they could revise their design to maximize efficiency.

Tip You may wish to conduct parts of this activity outside, as it involves students pouring water that may splash outside of their bucket.

Student Tip This lab will help you learn some of the advantages and disadvantages of using moving water as a source of energy.

Skills Focus Building Models, Collecting Data, Developing Procedures

MODIFICATION FOR GUIDED Inquiry

Narrow the scope of available materials by selecting five or six of the ones given for students to use, and require that they use at least three of them as they design a turbine. In this way, students will still be responsible for designing a model and developing some of the procedural steps, but in a more limited capacity.

MATERIALS

For each group
- bottle, 1L
- bottle, 2L
- bucket (same size for each group)
- card, index
- clay, modeling
- container, plastic
- craft sticks
- cup, clear plastic
- dowel, wooden
- film canister
- foam board
- glue, white
- hole punch
- rubber band
- scissors
- straw, plastic
- tape, duct
- thumbtack
- tube, cardboard
- water

For each student
- lab apron
- safety goggles

My Notes

_____

_____

_____

_____

_____

Answer Key

1. Accept all reasonable answers. Students' procedures should include how they will build and test a model turbine. For example, it may include a materials list and a brief description of how they will build the turbine (ex. We will use cardboard that freely spins around a wood dowel with three film canisters attached to catch the water.) Student responses should also include a labeled sketch of their design.

3. Sample answer: We will pour water over the turbine at a rate of 2 liters per 30 seconds.

5. Sample answer:

Trial	Number of revolutions
1	12
2	9
3	11
4	11
Average:	11

6. Accept all reasonable answers.

7. Accept all reasonable answers.

   Teacher Prompt If the rate of water pouring over your turbine remains the same, what could you change on your model to allow it to spin faster?

8. Accept all reasonable answers. Students should understand that the turbine is used to convert mechanical energy into electrical energy. The turbine would need to be connected to a generator to generate electricity that must then be carried through a transformer and a power grid to distribute the electricity for people to use.

9. Sample answer: There are advantages and disadvantages to the proposed hydroelectric power plant. An advantage is that water is a renewable resource, and hydroelectric power plants do not release pollutants. However, the town should consider the possible negative environmental impacts from building a dam that will likely change the rate of water flow downstream of the plant.

QUICK LAB INDEPENDENT *Inquiry*

Design a Turbine

A turbine is used to convert mechanical energy of a spinning blade into electrical energy. For example, wind turbines use moving air to supply the energy needed for the spinning action. Water turbines use falling water. In this lab, you will work with your group to design and build a model of a water turbine. You will test your turbine by pouring a specific volume of water over it in a specified time while counting the number of revolutions it makes.

PROCEDURE

① Work with your group to develop procedures for building a model of a water turbine. Write out the materials you will use, and include a sketch with labels of what the model will look like.

_____

_____

_____

② Have your teacher approve your model. If necessary, make any modifications. Then build your model turbine according to your plan.

③ Work with your class to decide on a rate at which you will pour water over your turbines. Every group should use the same amount of water poured for the same length of time. Write the rate below.

_____

④ Hold your turbine over the plastic tub (or, if allowed, go outside). While one member of the group is holding the turbine, another member will pour water over it. A third member of the group will count how many times the turbine spins as the water pours over it.

OBJECTIVES

- Understand that water is a renewable energy resource.
- Build and test a model of a simple water turbine.

MATERIALS

For each group
- bottle, 1L
- bottle, 2L
- bucket
- card, index
- clay, modeling
- container, plastic
- craft sticks
- cup, clear plastic
- dowel, wooden
- film canister
- foam board
- glue, white
- hole punch
- rubber band
- scissors
- straw, plastic
- tape, duct
- thumbtack
- tube, cardboard
- water

For each student
- lab apron
- safety goggles

Quick Lab continued

5 Repeat your trial three more times. Create a table in the space below to show the results of your trials. Calculate the average number of revolutions for your turbine and include that data in your table.

6 How did your results compare to those of the other groups in your class?

_____

_____

7 What improvements could you make to your model to make it more efficient?

_____

_____

_____

8 How would your model need to be modified to generate electricity similar to an actual hydroelectric plant?

_____

_____

_____

_____

9 A small town wants to generate some of its electricity using a nearby water source. The townspeople have plans to build a dam on the local river to produce a suitable water flow that could drive a water turbine. Discuss the advantages and disadvantages the town should consider before carrying out its plan.

_____

_____

_____

_____

QUICK LAB DIRECTED *Inquiry*

Understanding Solar Panels GENERAL

👥 Small groups

🕐 20 minutes

LAB RATINGS

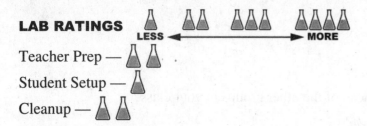

Teacher Prep —

Student Setup —

Cleanup —

MATERIALS

For each group

- clay, modeling (red or orange)
- cloth, black, 8 cm × 8 cm (2)
- cloth, white, 8 cm × 8 cm (2)
- foil, aluminum, 8 cm × 8 cm (2)
- glass, colored (green or blue)
- image of solar panel
- lamp, gooseneck
- stopwatch
- thermometer, alcohol

SAFETY INFORMATION

Remind students to review all safety cautions and icons before beginning this lab. Students should be instructed as to the proper handling of heated objects. They should use care when handling objects that have been exposed to heat. The objects in this lab are only under a heating lamp for one minute, but some objects still might become quite hot. Students should never touch heated items with their hands until the object has completely cooled. At the same time, students do need to experience warmth from the objects in order to judge which ones absorb the most heat, so gloves are not ideal unless you are concerned about students not following safety instructions. Have students use an alcohol thermometer that is either underneath the material or wrapped inside the material. They should not use their hands to determine how much heat has been absorbed.

My Notes

_____

_____

_____

_____

_____

TEACHER NOTES

In this activity, students will conduct simple tests to understand the function and design of solar panels. They will set different materials under a lamp for one minute, then record the temperature to determine which ones absorb the most heat. This lab will help students understand the design of solar panels.

Skills Focus Making Observations, Practicing Lab Techniques, Applying Concepts

MODIFICATION FOR GUIDED *Inquiry*

Provide students with the same materials, but challenge them to devise their own methods for testing how the materials behave when exposed to heat and light.

Answer Key

2. Sample answer: The foil was warm, but not hot.

3. Sample answer: The foil ball was much cooler than the foil sheet. We were able to touch it right away.
Teacher Prompt What changed to make the foil feel cooler this time?

4. Accept all reasonable answers.

5. Accept all reasonable answers.

6. Accept all reasonable answers.

7. Accept all reasonable answers.

8. Sample answer: The black cloth was hotter than the white cloth because black objects absorb more heat than white objects.
Teacher Prompt Which was hotter: the white cloth or the black cloth? Why?

9. Accept all reasonable answers.

10. Sample answer: The black cloth became the hottest. It was hotter when it was lying flat than when it was crumpled. This is because black objects tend to absorb more heat than light-colored objects. The flat objects absorbed heat more uniformly than the wrinkled or crumpled objects.

11. Accept all reasonable answers. Students should understand that when the shape of the object was flat under the light, it could absorb heat more uniformly than when it was wrinkled or crumpled.

12. Sample answer: Solar panels are black and flat. This makes sense because in this lab, I observed that darker colors absorbed more heat, as did the flatter objects.

13. Accept all reasonable answers. Students should understand that solar panels are not the best choice for locations that do not receive much sunlight.

14. Sample answer: Solar panels would be most effective in a sunny area like a desert because there is ample sunlight to collect.

15. Sample answer: The solar panel needs to have sunlight shining on it in order to work. So, in a crowded neighborhood, a solar panel might work best on the roof.

16. Accept all reasonable answers. Students should describe a process by which they would model a solar panel that moves with the changing levels of sunlight.

Understanding Solar Panels

In this lab, you will conduct simple tests to help you understand why solar panels look the way they do. You will apply your observations from this lab to scenarios about solar panels so that you can understand both the advantages and disadvantages to using the renewable resource of sunlight.

PROCEDURE

1 Set up your gooseneck lamp on the table so that the light is angled downward, as shown in the image below.

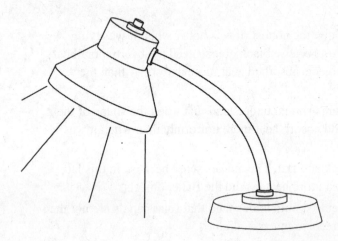

2 Place the flat sheet of aluminum foil under the lamp for one minute. Carefully feel the foil and record your observations.

_____

3 Now, wrinkle the second sheet of aluminum foil into a ball and place it under the lamp for one minute. Record your observations. Compare these results with your observations in Step 2.

_____

4 Shape the modeling clay into a flat surface. Place it under the lamp for one minute. Record your observations.

_____

OBJECTIVES

- Understand the design of solar panels.
- Explain how solar energy is harnessed.
- Test how different materials absorb heat.

MATERIALS

For each group

- clay, modeling (red or orange)
- cloth, black, 8 cm × 8 cm (2)
- cloth, white, 8 cm × 8 cm (2)
- foil, aluminum, 8 cm × 8 cm (2)
- glass, colored (green or blue)
- image of solar panel
- lamp, gooseneck
- stopwatch
- thermometer, alcohol

Quick Lab continued

5 Place the colored glass under the lamp for one minute. Record your observations.

_____

6 Place the white cloth flat under the lamp for one minute. Record your observations.

_____

7 Wrinkle the second sheet of white cloth so that it has many bumps and ridges. Place it under the lamp for one minute. Record your observations.

_____

8 Place the black cloth flat under the lamp for one minute. Record your observations. Compare these results with your observations in Step 6.

_____

9 Wrinkle the second sheet of black cloth so that it has many bumps and ridges. Place it under the lamp for one minute. Record your observations.

_____

10 Which object became the hottest after one minute under the lamp? Why?

_____

_____

11 How did the shape of the object under the lamp affect how much heat it absorbed?

_____

_____

12 Look at the image of the solar panel. Using your observations from this lab, explain why the solar panel is designed the way that it is.

_____

_____

Quick Lab continued

13 What possible drawbacks could there be to using solar panels in an area with little sunlight?

_____

_____

14 What possible advantages could there be to using solar panels in a sunny, desert-like area?

_____

_____

15 Imagine that you lived in a neighborhood with many houses built close together. Where might the best place be to install solar panels?

_____

_____

16 Some solar panels are designed to move with the sun. They change position during the day as the sun moves across the sky. They also change position from season to season, tilting so that they receive the maximum amount of sunlight. How could you model this type of solar panel using the materials in this lab?

_____

_____

_____

_____

S.T.E.M. LAB DIRECTED Inquiry **AND** GUIDED Inquiry

Modeling Geothermal Power GENERAL

👥 Small groups

🕐 45 minutes

LAB RATINGS

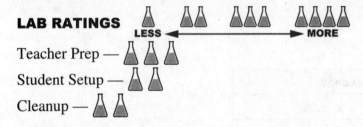

LESS ←————————→ MORE

Teacher Prep —

Student Setup —

Cleanup —

SAFETY INFORMATION

Remind students to review all safety cautions and icons before beginning this lab. Students should always use caution when working with a hot plate. In this lab, the heat resistant glass beaker must become hot enough to produce steam; that steam will be very hot and can cause burns, so students must use extreme caution. Caution students to monitor the water as it heats in the beaker. The water should be hot enough to produce steam, but it should not be so hot that it begins to boil.

TEACHER NOTES

In this activity, students will build a model turbine using the materials provided. The shoeboxes collected should be narrow enough for a pencil to fit through. They will place a beaker of water on a hot plate to generate steam. They will use books to position the model turbine in the steam and count how many times the turbine spins in a set amount of time. You will need to create a turbine pattern on the poster board prior to the activity. To do this, simply draw an "X" on each poster board square.

Tip Make sure your students are well-versed in the proper lab techniques for working with a hot plate and handling potentially hot objects.

Student Tip This lab will help you model how geothermal energy works. Keep in mind that a spinning turbine in a geothermal power plant is used to generate electricity by its spinning motion.

Skills Focus Creating Models, Practicing Lab Techniques

MODIFICATION FOR INDEPENDENT Inquiry

Present students with a challenge, such as, "How can you create a model to show how to capture and use geothermal energy?" Have students brainstorm a list of materials and the procedure that they will use. You may still wish to provide students with the turbine pattern as presented in this lab.

MATERIALS

For each group

- beaker, heat-resistant glass
- books (5–6)
- clay, modeling
- hole punch
- hot plate
- marker, permanent
- pencil, round
- pipe cleaners (2)
- poster board (10 x 10 cm square, with turbine pattern)
- ruler
- scissors
- shoe box
- stopwatch
- tape
- thumbtack

For each student

- safety goggles

My Notes

_____

_____

_____

_____

_____

S.T.E.M. Lab continued

Answer Key for DIRECTED Inquiry

FORM A PREDICTION

11. Accept all reasonable answers. Students should understand that the turbine will spin when the steam hits it, though the actual number of rotations may vary widely.

TEST THE PREDICTION

13. Sample answer:

Trial #	Rotations in 30 seconds
1	9
2	15
3	17
4	19
5	22
	Average rotations = 16.4

ANALYZE THE RESULTS

14. Sample answer: The poster board is very thick and needs quite a bit of steam to rotate. Also, after several trials, the thumbtack became loose and we had to make a few adjustments.

15. Accept all reasonable answers. If time allows, permit students to make the changes they brainstormed and conduct another set of trials, similar to Steps 12 and 13.

16. Sample answer: We adjusted where the steam was hitting the turbine. In the first trial, the steam hit the turbine head on, and the turbine didn't rotate much. In the later trials, we shifted the turbine so that it received the steam at an angle, which helped it spin better.

17. Accept all reasonable answers.

DRAW CONCLUSIONS

18. In places where the steam or water reaches Earth's surface, such as geysers and hot springs.
Teacher Prompt How would you know if geothermal energy is used in our area? What are some places in the United States that use geothermal energy? Why do you think the country of Iceland uses so much geothermal energy?

19. Earth's core will be hot for billions of years so geothermal energy will be available for a long time. This is an advantage, making it a cost-effective energy resource. The disadvantage is that it is not accessible everywhere. In some places, it is located too deep within Earth to make it cost-effective to access.

S.T.E.M. Lab continued

Connect TO THE ESSENTIAL QUESTION

20. Sample answer: Geothermal energy can help society by providing power without generating pollution from the power plant. It can be used to warm homes and buildings.

Answer Key for GUIDED Inquiry

BUILD A MODEL

6. Sample answer: To make one blade of the turbine stand out, we will color it a different color.

8. Accept all reasonable answers. Students should describe a method to make the blades of the turbine match up with the steam from the beaker, such as stacking the model on top of a few books.

FORM A PREDICTION

9. Students should understand that the turbine will spin when the steam hits it, though the actual numbers of rotations may vary widely.

TEST THE PREDICTION

11. Sample answer:

Trial #	Rotations in 30 seconds
1	9
2	15
3	17
4	19
5	22
	Average rotations = 16.4

ANALYZE THE RESULTS

12. Sample answer: The poster board is very thick and needs quite a bit of steam to rotate. Also, after several trials, the thumbtack became loose and we had to make a few adjustments.

13. Accept all reasonable answers. If time allows, permit students to make the changes they brainstormed and conduct another set of trials, similar to Steps 12 and 13.

14. Sample answer: We adjusted where the steam was hitting the turbine. In the first trial, the steam hit the turbine head on, and the turbine didn't rotate much. In the later trials, we shifted the turbine so that it received the steam at an angle, which helped it spin better.

15. Accept all reasonable answers.

S.T.E.M. Lab continued

DRAW CONCLUSIONS

16. In places where the steam or water reaches Earth's surface, such as geysers and hot springs.

Teacher Prompt How would you know if geothermal energy is used in our area? What are some places in the United States that use geothermal energy? Why do you think the country of Iceland uses so much geothermal energy?

17. Earth's core will be hot for billions of years so geothermal energy will be available for a long time. This is an advantage, making it a cost-effective energy resource. The disadvantage is that it is not accessible everywhere. In some places, it is located too deep within Earth to make it cost-effective to access.

Connect TO THE ESSENTIAL QUESTION

18. Sample answer: Geothermal energy can help society by providing power without generating pollution from the power plant. It can be used to warm homes and buildings.

S.T.E.M. LAB DIRECTED *Inquiry*

Modeling Geothermal Power

In this lab, you will create a model turbine and attempt to power it using steam, which represents geothermal energy. You will collect data and brainstorm ways in which you could improve your design to make it more efficient. Geothermal energy is a renewable resource, but it does have some limitations, which you will also explore in this lab. Be sure to use extreme caution when working with steam, as it can cause serious burns.

PROCEDURE

BUILD A MODEL

1 Trace the turbine pattern your teacher will provide for you on your poster board. Punch a hole in the center of the poster board. Use scissors to cut along the trace lines almost to the center.

2 Slide the turbine onto the eraser end of the pencil. Bend the flaps of the turbine toward the eraser and attach them with the thumbtack, as shown in the image below. The turbine should rotate freely when you blow on it.

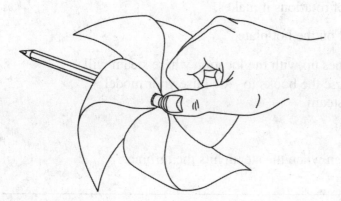

3 Tape the back end of the turbine to the pencil so that the turbine can no longer rotate unless the pencil rotates with it. Make sure the turbine blades remain curved so there is a lot of space to catch steam.

4 Place the shoe box on the table so that the opening faces up. Measure 7 centimeters (cm) up from the table on a long side of the box, and mark that point on the box. Punch a hole through the point.

OBJECTIVES
- Build a model to harness steam energy.
- Create a model turbine and power it using steam.

MATERIALS
For each group
- beaker, heat-resistant glass
- books (5–6)
- clay, modeling
- hole punch
- hot plate
- marker, permanent
- pencil, round
- pipe cleaners (2)
- poster board (10 x 10 cm square, with turbine pattern)
- ruler
- scissors
- shoe box
- stopwatch
- tape
- thumbtack
For each student
- safety goggles

S.T.E.M. Lab continued

5 Repeat Step 4 on the opposite side of the box so that the holes are aligned on both sides of the box.

6 Slide the pencil through the two holes so that the pencil is horizontal to the table and the turbine extends beyond the box, as shown in the image below. Cut the holes larger if the pencil does not rotate freely. Allow 3 to 4 cm of the pencil to stick out on the turbine side of the box.

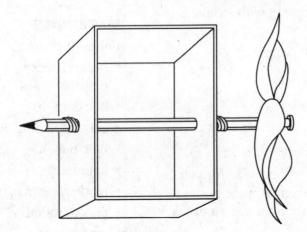

7 Wrap pipe cleaners around the pencil where it exits on both sides of the box. Tape the pipe cleaners to the pencil. They will allow the pencil to spin without accidentally sliding out of the box.

8 Use the permanent marker to make a mark on one of the turbine blades. This will help you count the number of rotations it makes.

9 Put water in the beaker and put it on the hot plate.

10 Position your turbine so that it lines up with the location where steam will escape the beaker. If necessary, use the books to   raise your model turbine so that it aligns with the steam.

FORM A PREDICTION

11 Predict what you think will happen when the steam hits the turbine.

_____

_____

S.T.E.M. Lab continued

TEST THE PREDICTION

⑫ Turn on the hot plate and wait until steam begins to form. When it does, start your stopwatch and count the number of times that the turbine spins in 30 seconds. Record your results in the table below.

_____

_____

⑬ Make any adjustments you deem necessary (such as changing the angle of the turbine as it relates to the steam), and repeat the trial four more times. Each time, record your results in the table below. When you have conducted five trials, compute the average number of rotations.

Trial #	Rotations in 30 seconds
	Average rotations =

ANALYZE THE RESULTS

⑭ **Identifying Constraints** What are some of the limitations of your model, or of its design?

_____

_____

⑮ **Evaluating Models** Work with your group to discuss ways you could improve your model to make it spin faster. If time allows, your teacher may ask you to make these changes and repeat your trials.

_____

_____

_____

Name _____ Class _____ Date _____

16 **Examining Methods** In Step 13 you adjusted your model to improve it. What changes did you make, and how did they affect how your turbine rotated?

_____

_____

_____

17 **Comparing Models** How did your model compare to the models made by other groups? Take a moment to share your results with the class, and reflect on why groups had similar or different results.

_____

_____

_____

DRAW CONCLUSIONS

18 **Applying Concepts** This lab simulated geothermal energy, the energy produced by heat within Earth. Where would you be likely to harness geothermal energy on Earth?

_____

_____

19 **Explaining Costs and Benefits** Why is geothermal energy considered a renewable resource? Describe at least one advantage and one disadvantage of using geothermal energy.

_____

_____

_____

_____

Connect TO THE ESSENTIAL QUESTION

20 **Applying Conclusions** How can a renewable resource like geothermal energy help society?

_____

_____

_____

_____

S.T.E.M. LAB GUIDED *Inquiry*

Modeling Geothermal Power

In this lab, you will create a model turbine and attempt to power it using steam, which represents geothermal energy. The materials and some of the procedures will be provided for you, but your group must also develop some procedural steps. You will collect data and brainstorm ways in which you could improve your design to make it more efficient. Geothermal energy is a renewable resource, but it does have some limitations, which you will also explore in this lab. Be sure to use extreme caution when working with steam as it can cause serious burns.

PROCEDURE

BUILD A MODEL

1 Trace the turbine pattern your teacher will provide for you on your poster board. Punch a hole in the center of the poster board. Use the scissors to cut along the trace lines almost to the center.

2 Slide the turbine onto the eraser end of the pencil. Bend the flaps of the turbine toward the eraser, and attach them with the thumbtack, as shown in the below image. The turbine should rotate freely when you blow on it. For additional support, add modeling clay to the eraser to help attach the turbine flaps to the pencil.

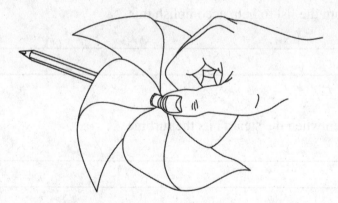

3 Tape the back end of the turbine to the pencil so that the turbine can no longer rotate unless the pencil rotates with it. Make sure the turbine blades remain curved so there is a lot of space to catch steam.

OBJECTIVES
- Build a model to harness steam energy.
- Create a model turbine and power it using steam.

MATERIALS

For each group
- beaker, heat-resistant glass
- books (5–6)
- clay, modeling
- hole punch
- hot plate
- marker, permanent
- pencil, round
- pipe cleaners (2)
- poster board (10 x 10 cm square, with turbine pattern)
- ruler
- scissors
- shoe box
- stopwatch
- tape
- thumbtack

For each student
- safety goggles

S.T.E.M. Lab continued

4 You will now need to insert the pencil into the shoe box. When you finish, it should look like the image below. Work with your group to decide what steps you will take and what materials you will use to make your model look like the one below.

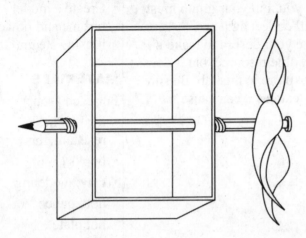

5 Wrap pipe cleaners around the pencil where it exits on both sides of the box. Tape the pipe cleaners to the pencil. They will allow the pencil to spin without accidentally sliding out of the box.

6 Develop a way to make one of the turbine blades stand out so that you will be able to count the number of rotations. Write your idea below, then alter your model as you described.

_____

_____

7 Put water in the beaker and place it on the hot plate.

8 How will you make the blades of your turbine line up with the steam from the beaker? Use any materials from the list to help accomplish this.

_____

_____

FORM A PREDICTION

9 Predict what you think will happen when the steam hits the turbine.

_____

_____

S.T.E.M. Lab continued

TEST THE PREDICTION

10 Turn on the hot plate and wait until steam begins to form. When it does, start your stopwatch and count the number of times that the turbine spins in thirty seconds. Record your results in the table you create (as described in the next step).

11 Make any adjustments you deem necessary (such as changing the angle of the turbine as it relates to the steam), and repeat the trial four more times. Create a table to display your results from each trial. When you have conducted five trials, compute the average number of rotations.

Trial #	Rotations in 30 seconds
	Average rotations =

ANALYZE THE RESULTS

12 **Identifying Constraints** What are some of the limitations of your model, or of its design?

_____

_____

13 **Evaluating Models** Work with your group to discuss ways you could improve your model to make it spin faster. If time allows, your teacher may ask you to make these changes and repeat your trials.

_____

_____

_____

14 **Examining Methods** Step 11 asked you to make slight changes to your model to improve it. What changes did you make, and how did they affect how your turbine rotated?

_____

_____

_____

S.T.E.M. Lab continued

15 **Comparing Models** How did your model compare to the models made by other groups? Take a moment to share your results with the class, and reflect on why groups had similar or different results.

_____

_____

_____

DRAW CONCLUSIONS

16 **Applying Concepts** This lab simulated geothermal energy, the energy produced by heat within Earth. Where would you be likely to harness geothermal energy on Earth?

_____

_____

17 **Explaining Costs and Benefits** Why is geothermal energy considered a renewable resource? Describe at least one advantage and one disadvantage of using geothermal energy.

_____

_____

_____

_____

Connect TO THE ESSENTIAL QUESTION

18 **Applying Conclusions** How can a renewable resource like geothermal energy help society?

_____

_____

_____

_____

QUICK LAB   DIRECTED Inquiry

Managing a Resource GENERAL

👥 Small groups
🕐 25 minutes

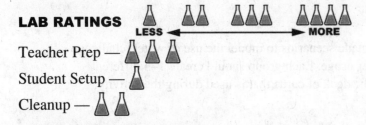

LAB RATINGS

LESS ← → MORE

Teacher Prep —

Student Setup —

Cleanup —

SAFETY INFORMATION

Remind students to review all safety cautions and icons before beginning this lab. Show students how to use a buret so that they can control the flow of water by turning the stopcock. Warn students to be careful not to tip over the graduated cylinder when filling it.

TEACHER NOTES

In this activity, students will model the management of freshwater as a resource. They will use water in a buret to model the different ways it can be used and conserved. Each group will have a stack of 10–12 index cards, each with a different scenario. Each card will represent a one-month period; ideally, your students will model a one-year period of time. When students draw a card, they will be presented with a scenario that may affect the rate of use of the resource. Both positive and negative effects are possible. You will need to create these scenario cards before the activity. If possible, have enough scenarios so that groups will have different outcomes at the end of the activity. Some sample scenarios are shown below.

Sample scenarios:

- An increase in demand for plastics has increased water usage by a factor of two.
- A bill passed by the legislature to limit dumping of industrial waste into natural waters means that the rate of use of freshwater will slow by half.
- More people are buying showerheads that cut the rate of water flow when they shower. Water consumption decreases by 0.5 milliliters (mL) per month.
- Farmers are attending educational seminars that provide them with alternatives to pesticides and fertilizers. Contamination of freshwater resources decreases and rate slows by 1.5 mL per month.
- An inventor finds a way to desalinate large amounts of ocean water using solar energy. Replenish your water supply at a rate of 2 mL per month.
- A fish that lives in your town's reservoir has been identified as endangered, and water usage has been restricted to aid its survival. Water consumption decreases by 0.5 mL per month.
- New housing developments are built, adding an additional 1000 families to your town. Water consumption increases by 1 mL per month.
- Water usage remains unchanged for one month, and usage stays at 2 mL.

MATERIALS

For each group
- buret, 50 mL
- buret stand and clamp
- cards, index, with scenarios (10–12)
- cylinder, graduated, 100 mL
- water

For each student
- lab apron
- safety goggles

My Notes

_____

_____

_____

_____

_____

Quick Lab continued

Tip As you create your scenarios for your students, incorporate local and regional examples whenever possible. If you do not have burets available, use a funnel outfitted with flexible tubing and a pinch clamp. Students will still collect their water in a graduated cylinder to measure it.

Student Tip The water in your buret represents the freshwater supply for your region, and the typical rate of 2 mL per month represents the amount of freshwater used by all users in the region.

Skills Focus Practicing Lab Techniques, Recording Data, Recognizing Outcomes

MODIFICATION FOR GUIDED *Inquiry*

Rather than providing students with teacher-made scenarios to model the use of water, challenge them to create their own scenarios about water usage. Each group should create 1–3 different scenarios. These can then be combined into the deck of cards that is used during the activity.

Answer Key

4. Sample answer:

USE OF FRESHWATER RESOURCE

Round #	Amount of water in buret at start of round (mL)	Amount of water in buret at end of round (mL)
1	50.0	48.0
2	48.0	44.0
3	44.0	45.5
4	45.5	45.5
5	45.5	40.0
6	40.0	38.0
7	38.0	40.0
8	40.0	36.0
9	36.0	34.0
10	34.0	35.0

5. Accept all reasonable answers. Students should identify the uses that caused their group to use more than 2 mL a month (the base rate amount described in procedure Step 2).

6. Accept all reasonable answers. Students should identify the uses that caused their group to use less than 2 mL a month (the base rate amount described in procedure Step 2).

7. Sample answer: Modeling is useful for observing how water usage impacts a water resource. Modeling as many scenarios as possible can help us to anticipate, prepare for, and possibly prevent overuse of water resources.

8. Accept all reasonable answers.
Teacher Prompt How will your management solutions be different when you are managing a resource on a large scale, like globally, versus a small scale, like your local town?

QUICK LAB DIRECTED *Inquiry*

Managing a Resource

In this lab, you will model the management of freshwater. You will have a buret filled with water and a set of cards with possible water use scenarios. Each card represents a one-month period. You will follow the instructions on your card and keep track of how freshwater is used.

PROCEDURE

1 Fill your buret to the top line. Make sure the stopcock at the bottom of the buret is closed so that no water escapes. Place the 100 mL graduated cylinder underneath the buret to catch water.

2 In this activity, you will model different water use scenarios. For this activity, a typical month will use 2 mL of water. Remove 2 mL of water from your buret each round to show a typical month. Let the water drain into your graduated cylinder. If too much drains out of the buret, pour it back into the buret until you have 2 mL remaining in the graduated cylinder.

3 Draw one card from your deck of cards and read the scenario. Each scenario describes the water use for one month. Work with your group to decide how you will model the situation on the card. Will you add more water or remove water? Write down the changes in the table below. The changes will include a typical month's water usage and any changes described by the scenario.

4 Repeat Step three until you have modeled the scenarios on all of your cards. As you work, fill out the table below.

OBJECTIVES

- Observe changing levels of a resource as a result of human use.
- Model the management of a resource to see how various situations affect its rate of depletion.

MATERIALS

- buret, 50 mL
- buret stand and clamp
- cards, index, with scenarios (10–12)
- cylinder, graduated, 100 mL
- water

For each student
- lab apron
- safety goggles

USE OF FRESHWATER RESOURCE

Round #	Amount of water in buret at start of round (mL)	Amount of water in buret at end of round (mL)
1		
2		
3		
4		
5		
6		
7		
8		
9		
10		

Quick Lab continued

5 In which scenarios did your group need to use more water?

_____

_____

_____

_____

6 In which scenarios was your group able to use less water?

_____

_____

_____

_____

7 Why is it important to model how different scenarios can affect the rate of freshwater usage?

_____

_____

_____

8 Work with your group to brainstorm at least two ways to manage resources at a local level, two ways to manage resources at a national level, and two ways to manage resources at a global level. Your responses can be related to freshwater, or you can think about another resource that needs management.

_____

_____

_____

_____

_____

_____

_____

QUICK LAB INDEPENDENT *Inquiry*

The Impact of Resource Extraction GENERAL

👥 Small groups
🕐 20 minutes

LAB RATINGS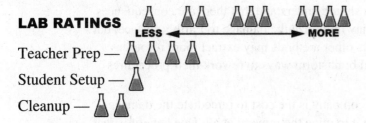
LESS ◄————► MORE

Teacher Prep —

Student Setup —

Cleanup —

MATERIALS

For each group
• knives, plastic
• pan of gelatin containing raisins
• spoons, plastic
• stopwatch
• straws
• toothpicks

For each student
• gloves
• lab apron
• safety goggles

SAFETY INFORMATION

Remind students to review all safety cautions and icons before beginning this lab. Warn students not to eat the raisins they extract from the gelatin. Have students wash and dry their hands upon completion of this inquiry.

TEACHER NOTES

In this activity, students will model extracting a resource by using simple tools to extract raisins from a pan of gelatin. You will need to make several pans of gelatin ahead of time, one per group, and allow sufficient time for the gelatin to set completely. Challenge students to develop their own procedures with limited teacher instruction, but observe as they work to answer questions or offer tips as needed. Stop students after 10 minutes have passed. As students are counting the raisins they extracted, circulate among groups and count each disturbance. This will be the basis for the fine you charge each group (for example, six disturbances to the surface of the gelatin equals a $300 fine).

Tip Your students will be encouraged to attach real world significance to this activity when you attach a monetary value to both the raisins and any disturbances they create on the surface of the gelatin.

Student Tip Think about natural resources you use in your life that are extracted from Earth.

Skills Focus Manipulating Models, Developing Procedures

MODIFICATION FOR GUIDED *Inquiry*

Begin the activity by showing students possible ways to use the materials to extract raisins from the pan. For example, show them that the toothpick creates very little disturbance on the surface of the pan, but cannot easily extract the raisin. The spoon, on the other hand, can easily scoop out the raisins but creates a large disturbance. Once you have modeled the tools, allow students to proceed with the activity as described in the procedures.

My Notes

_____

_____

_____

_____

_____

Answer Key

3. Accept all reasonable answers. Students should understand, even before extracting raisins, that some tools will extract raisins faster but will cause a greater impact. Student plans should identify steps or a process for extraction and may include test runs of various tools.

5. Sample answer: We extracted 14 raisins and created 9 disturbances.

6. Sample answer: My group gained $250.

7. Accept all reasonable answers. Students should understand that there are consequences to extraction methods. Some methods may minimize the damage to Earth's surface, but may not extract as many resources, while other methods may extract more resources but cause more damage. Students should brainstorm ways to rework their procedures to improve their outcome.

8. Sample answer: One cost to the mining company is the cost to remediate the damage caused by mining. It might not be worth it to mine the mineral at all. One benefit is that the mineral may be worth more than the money it costs to extract and remediate, so the company could make a profit.

Teacher Prompt What are the costs and benefits associated with mining?

QUICK LAB

The Impact of Resource Extraction

In this lab, you will model the impacts of resource extraction by "mining" raisins from a pan of gelatin. By successfully removing raisins, your group can gain rewards, but you will also receive penalties if you disturb the gelatin too much! You will work with your group to devise the best method for extraction.

PROCEDURE

1 Your teacher will provide you with a pan with gelatin. You'll notice raisins in the gelatin. The gelatin represents Earth's surface. The raisins represent natural resources that can be extracted from Earth. You will also receive a few other materials that you can use to extract the raisins from the gelatin.

2 You will work with your group to extract the resource. For each raisin you extract, you will receive 50 (imaginary) dollars. Additionally, each disturbance to the gelatin will cost your group 50 (imaginary) dollars.

3 You will have 10 minutes to extract as many raisins as possible while minimizing the disturbances to the gelatin. Work with your group to devise a plan to extract the raisins. Write your plan below. Sketch an image if necessary.

_____

_____

_____

_____

_____

4 When your teacher tells you to start, begin extracting the raisins. Your teacher will tell you when the 10 minutes are up.

5 Count up the number of raisins you successfully extracted. Write this number below. While you are working, your teacher will come around and assess a fine based on the number of disturbances to the gelatin you created. Write this number below.

_____

_____

OBJECTIVE
• Model resource extraction to better understand some of the impacts of extraction processes.

MATERIALS
• knives, plastic
• pan of gelatin containing raisins
• spoons, plastic
• straws
• toothpicks
For each student
• gloves
• lab apron
• safety goggles

Quick Lab continued

6 How much money did you gain or lose?

_____

7 Explain why your group was successful or unsuccessful. What could you change if you were to repeat this activity?

_____

_____

_____

_____

_____

_____

8 A mining company wants to extract a valuable mineral from land in a sensitive ecological habitat. What are some of the costs and benefits that the mining company should consider?

_____

_____

_____

_____

QUICK LAB DIRECTED *Inquiry*

Ocean Pollution from Land GENERAL

👥 Small groups

🕐 20 minutes

LAB RATINGS

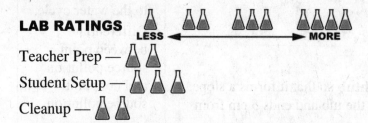

LESS ⟵————⟶ MORE

Teacher Prep —

Student Setup —

Cleanup —

SAFETY INFORMATION

Remind students to review all safety cautions and icons before beginning this lab. Warn students that sand can cause serious eye damage. Spilled materials should be cleaned up immediately to prevent slipping hazards.

TEACHER NOTES

In this activity, students will build a model that shows how the water cycle helps land pollution enter bodies of water, such as the ocean. Note that in the procedure, coarse sand must be used because fine or medium sand holds the color and doesn't allow it to wash through.

Skills Focus Making Models, Applying Concepts, Evaluating Models

MODIFICATION FOR GUIDED *Inquiry*

Provide students with a list of materials, and have students brainstorm ways of modeling the movement of pollution from land to water. Allow students to perform all reasonable experiments. Encourage them to share their conclusions with the class.

MATERIALS

For each group
- food coloring, red and blue (3–4 drops each)
- sand, coarse, wet (1/3 volume of washtub)
- spray bottle
- washtub, plastic
- water

For each student
- gloves
- lab apron
- safety goggles

My Notes

_____

_____

_____

_____

_____

Answer Key

4. Sample answer: The water that collected at the bottom of the basin has food coloring in it. It looks purple.

5. Sample answer: Pollution can be carried from land to the ocean by rain and runoff.

6. Sample answer: This is nonpoint source pollution because food coloring placed at any point can be washed into the model ocean.

7. Sample answer: This model is different from the real world because the model is much smaller than a watershed is, and there is no soil or plants. However, the model is a useful representation of how pollution on land can mix and wash into the ocean.

QUICK LAB DIRECTED *Inquiry*

Ocean Pollution from Land

In this lab, you will use a model of the ocean to demonstrate how pollution on land can become pollution in water. You will use sand to represent land, and tap water to represent the ocean.

PROCEDURE

1 Arrange **wet sand** in a **plastic washtub** so that it forms a slope that begins at the top of one end of the tub and ends 5 cm from the other end of the tub.

2 On the sand, place 3–4 drops of **red food coloring** toward the upper part of the slope.

3 Place three to four drops of **blue food coloring** toward the upper part of the slope.

4 Use a **spray bottle** filled with **water** to spray water toward the top of the slope. Continue to spray until water begins to collect at the low end of the slope. Write your observations below.

_____

_____

_____

_____

5 How is ocean pollution related to the water cycle?

_____

_____

_____

_____

_____

OBJECTIVES

- Explain how water pollution is related to the water cycle.
- Differentiate between point source pollution and nonpoint source pollution.

MATERIALS

For each group
- food coloring, blue (3–4 drops)
- food coloring, red (3–4 drops)
- sand, coarse, wet (1/3 volume of washtub)
- spray bottle
- washtub, plastic
- water

For each student
- gloves
- lab apron
- safety goggles

Quick Lab continued

6 Does this model represent point source pollution or nonpoint source pollution? Explain your answer.

_____

_____

_____

_____

_____

_____

7 How well does this model approximate pollution in the real world?

_____

_____

_____

_____

_____

_____

_____

Turbidity and Water Temperature GENERAL

👥 Small groups
🕐 30 minutes

LAB RATINGS

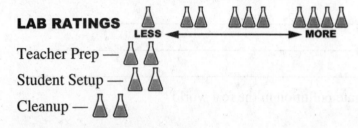

LESS ←———————→ MORE

Teacher Prep —

Student Setup —

Cleanup —

MATERIALS

For each group
- clear plastic cups (3)
- dirt or potting soil (about 3 tablespoons)
- marker
- spoon
- thermometer
- water (2 cups)

For each student
- gloves
- lab apron
- safety goggles

SAFETY INFORMATION

Remind students to review all safety cautions and icons before beginning this lab. If plastic cups are torn, their jagged or sharp edges may present a cutting hazard. Students should use caution and take care not to tear the cups, and they should dispose of any torn cups immediately. Water can cause a slipping hazard. Clean up all spills immediately.

TEACHER NOTES

In this activity, students will describe the effects of turbidity on water temperature. Turbidity is a measure of suspended solids in water. Turbid water is often cloudy or dark.

Water samples need to be placed in direct sunlight for 20 minutes. Make sure you have access to a sunny spot large enough to accommodate all the cups. Heat lamps can be used if a sunny area is not available. To dispose of water samples, scoop out solid material and throw it in the garbage, and pour water down the drain.

Skills Focus Making Observations, Making Inferences

MODIFICATION FOR INDEPENDENT *Inquiry*

Have students identify a question related to water turbidity, propose a hypothesis, and develop an experimental design to test their hypothesis. Their procedures should include all necessary materials and a method for data collection and analysis. With your approval, students should carry out any reasonable experiments and present their results to the class.

My Notes

_____

_____

_____

_____

_____

Answer Key

6. Answers will vary.

7. Sample answer: The temperature of turbid water increases more than the temperature of clear water when exposed to heat.

8. Sample answer: Erosion and storm runoff might make a river turbid.

9. Sample answer: Warmer, turbid water might be harmful to organisms and plants that need cold, clear water to survive. Turbid water might clog gills and block sunlight from underwater plants.

Turbidity and Water Temperature

In this lab, you will explore water quality issues by investigating how turbidity affects water temperature. You will use cups of water with different levels of turbidity to determine how water temperature is related to turbidity.

PROCEDURE

1 Use a **marker** to label three **clear plastic cups** "water," "1 spoonful," and "2 spoonfuls."

2 Fill each cup 2/3 full with **water.**

3 Use a **spoon** to stir one spoonful of **dirt** or **potting soil** into the cup labeled "1 spoonful."

4 Use a spoon to stir two spoonfuls of dirt or potting soil into the cup labeled "2 spoonfuls."

5 Place all three cups in a sunny spot.

6 Use a **thermometer** to record the temperatures of the water in all the cups at the beginning, after 10 minutes, and after 20 minutes. Record your results in the table below.

OBJECTIVE

- Describe the effect of turbidity on water temperature.

MATERIALS

For each group
- clear plastic cups (3)
- dirt or potting soil (about 3 tablespoons)
- marker
- spoon
- thermometer
- water (2 cups)

For each student
- gloves
- lab apron
- safety goggles

	Temperature at start (°F)	Temperature after 10 minutes (°F)	Temperature after 20 minutes (°F)
water			
1 spoonful			
2 spoonfuls			

Quick Lab continued

7 What is the relationship between turbidity and water temperature?

_____

_____

_____

_____

_____

8 How might clear water become turbid?

_____

_____

_____

_____

_____

_____

_____

_____

9 What might be some of the harmful results of increased turbidity and a change in temperature?

_____

_____

_____

_____

_____

_____

FIELD LAB GUIDED *Inquiry* **AND** INDEPENDENT *Inquiry*

Investigating Water Quality GENERAL

👥 Student pairs

🕐 Two 45-minute class periods

LAB RATINGS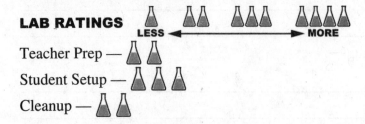

Teacher Prep —

Student Setup —

Cleanup —

MATERIALS

For each pair
- bottles (4)
- cups, clear plastic
- garden fertilizer
- marker
- measuring spoons
- pH meter or pH paper
- water samples

For each student
- lab apron
- safety goggles

SAFETY INFORMATION

Remind students to review all safety cautions and icons before beginning this lab. If students are collecting water from natural sources such as rivers or ponds, caution students to use care, especially if the student is unable to swim. Instruct students to use care to avoid harmful plants around water sources. Untreated water may carry toxins or disease. Students should be cautioned not drink untreated water.

Consider students' accessibility to the water source if it is a natural pond or stream. Students should wear appropriate protective footwear, such as an old pair of sneakers, if they need to wade into the water. The stream bed might consist of algae-covered stones that can present a slip hazard, or sharp-edges stones or submerged glass or metal. In these cases, your or a teaching assistant can collect water samples from these locations. If the water source is domestic or commercial water that may contain sewage, chemicals or potential pathogens, students should not be allowed to come in contact with this water.

Have paper towels available to clean up spilled water. Students should wash their hands after completing the lab.

My Notes

_____

_____

_____

_____

_____

TEACHER NOTES

This activity demonstrates to students that not all water samples are equal. The student obtains samples of water from various sources. These are characterized initially by pH and turbidity/clarity. Odor may also be used as a subjective observation. An equal amount of the fertilizer is added to each sample. Some fertilizers come in concentrated form. Use the suggested concentration in the instructions as a guide when assisting students. Over one or two weeks, the student will observe the changes in the water. The nitrogen will encourage growth of photosynthetic microorganisms. Turbidity will increase most in the samples with the highest initial density of microorganisms. The student will also learn about the principle of eutrophication since the lab shows how relatively clean water will be made turbid as microorganism growth rate is enhanced by the addition of a nitrogen source.

Tip This activity will help the student understand that water from different sources varies in quality and chemistry.

Skills Focus Practicing Lab Techniques, Devising Procedures, Drawing Conclusions

Field Lab continued

MODIFICATION FOR DIRECTED Inquiry

For a Directed Inquiry option, students can be directed to use specific sources of water, and data tables may be supplied for students to fill in rather than having students develop their own.

Answer Key for GUIDED Inquiry

DEVELOP A PLAN

2. Accept all reasonable answers. Be sure that students have included at least two natural water samples such as rain water and pond water, as well as two samples from commercial or human-treated sources such as bottled water and tap water.

MAKE OBSERVATIONS

4. Accept all reasonable answers. Check student data tables to be sure they are complete and well-organized before students begin collecting data.

6. Accept all reasonable answers. Any quantity between ¼ teaspoon to 2 teaspoons of fertilizer per cup of water is a reasonable amount for students to use.

7. Accept all reasonable answers. Check student data tables to be sure they are complete and well-organized before students begin collecting data.

ANALYZE THE RESULTS

8. Sample answer: The rain water had a lower pH than the other samples. The pond water was murkier than rainwater or tap water.

9. Sample answer: The bottled water and tap water became only barely cloudy in the last few days of the experiment with the added fertilizer, but the pond water became very thick and cloudy early on and got more and more cloudy with time.

DRAW CONCLUSIONS

10. Sample answer: The tap water, bottled water, and rain water were more similar in appearance and odor than the pond water, which was much cloudier and had a definite odor not detected in the other water samples. The pond water probably has microorganisms in it that make it look cloudy and give off wastes that cause the odor.

11. Sample answer: The pond water became murkier more quickly because it contained microorganisms whose growth was stimulated by light. This is confirmed because the pond water in the darkened area did not change as much.
Teacher Prompt What might be in the pond water that gives it a murky appearance?

Connect TO THE ESSENTIAL QUESTION

12. Applying Concepts Excess fertilizer ends up in natural waters because it gets carried there when rain and ground water carries the fertilizer from the farm fields into streams, ponds, and rivers. The fertilizer may cause an increase in microbial growth, which can change the amount of oxygen available in the water. This can affect the growth of plants and animals in those natural waters.

Answer Key for INDEPENDENT Inquiry

DEVELOP A PLAN

2. Accept all reasonable answers. Be sure that students have included at least two natural water samples such as rain water and pond water, as well as two samples from commercial or human-treated sources such as bottled water and tap water.

3. Accept all reasonable answers. Check student data tables to be sure they are complete and well-organized before students begin collecting data.

4. Accept all reasonable answers. Check student data tables to be sure they are complete and well-organized before students begin collecting data.

ANALYZE THE RESULTS

8. Sample answer: The rain water had a lower pH than the other samples. The pond water was murkier than rainwater or tap water.

9. Sample answer: The bottled water and tap water became only barely cloudy in the last few days of the experiment with the added fertilizer, but the pond water became very thick and cloudy early on and got more and more cloudy with time.

DRAW CONCLUSIONS

10. Sample answer: The tap water, bottled water, and rain water were more similar in appearance and odor than the pond water, which was much cloudier and had a definite odor not detected in the other water samples. The pond water probably has microorganisms in it that make it look cloudy and give off wastes that cause the odor.

11. Sample answer: The pond water became murkier more quickly because it contained microorganisms whose growth was stimulated by light. This is confirmed because the pond water in the darkened area did not change as much.
Teacher Prompt What might be in the pond water that gives it a murky appearance?

Connect TO THE ESSENTIAL QUESTION

12. Applying Concepts Excess fertilizer ends up in natural waters because it gets carried there when rain and ground water carries the fertilizer from the farm fields into streams, ponds, and rivers. The fertilizer may cause an increase in microbial growth, which can change the amount of oxygen available in the water. This can affect the growth of plants and animals in those natural waters.

FIELD LAB GUIDED *Inquiry*

Investigating Water Quality

In this lab you will collect samples of water from various locations and compare their chemical and biological properties. Then you will conduct a test to see how each sample changes over time after adding a small amount of garden fertilizer.

Use caution when collecting water samples from a natural source such as a lake, river, or pond. If you cannot swim, ask an adult to collect the samples for you. Use care to avoid harmful plants around water sources.

PROCEDURE

ASK A QUESTION

❶ In this lab, you will investigate the following questions: How does the quality of water vary from different sources? How does fertilizer runoff affect water quality?

DEVELOP A PLAN

❷ Work with your partner to decide what sources of water you will include in your survey of water quality. Be sure that you include at least two natural sources and two sources that are either commercial or treated by humans. Write your plan below for each source of water that you plan to survey.

_____

_____

_____

_____

_____

MAKE OBSERVATIONS

❸ Collect and label the water samples in clean, dry plastic cups and return to the lab.

OBJECTIVES

• Survey the quality of water taken from a variety of sources.

• Investigate the effects of adding garden fertilizer to different water samples.

MATERIALS

For each pair
• bottles (4)
• cups, clear plastic
• garden fertilizer
• marker
• measuring spoons
• pH meter or pH paper
• water samples

For each student
• lab apron
• safety goggles

Field Lab continued

④ Test each sample for pH (acidity), clarity, and odor using the following procedures.

   a. Label a clean, dry cup with the name of the sample and the date collected. Repeat for all samples. Place enough water from each sample to half-fill the cups.

   b. Place the samples close to a light source or hold them up to the sky. Observe the clarity of each water sample. Record your observations in your notebook.

   c. Smell each of the samples. Record your observations in your notebook.

   d. Use a pH meter or pH paper to determine each sample's pH. Record the data in a data table in the space below.

⑤ Set up samples for the fertilizer investigation. Do this by preparing control and experimental cups for each water sample you collected in Step 3. Be sure all cups are clearly labeled.

⑥ Decide on an amount of fertilizer to add to each experimental cup. Write that amount below.

_____

Field Lab continued

7 Cover the samples and place them in a location where they will not be disturbed. Over the next two to three weeks, check these at regular intervals and record your observations each time. Prepare a data table below that you will use to record your observations. Be sure to include a space to note the days on which you make your observations.

ANALYZE THE RESULTS

8 **Comparing Samples** What results did you obtain as a result of your survey of water quality? Did you observe any differences in the water samples? Did the clarity, pH, or odor differ among the water samples you studied?

_____

_____

_____

_____

9 **Analyzing Observations** What results did you obtain from the experiment in which you added fertilizer to the water samples? Did the different samples all undergo the same changes in response to the fertilizer, or did some change more than others?

DRAW CONCLUSIONS

10 **Comparing Results** If you observed differences in the water samples during your initial survey, what could account for those differences? Explain.

_____

_____

_____

_____

Field Lab continued

11 **Comparing Results** If you observed differences in the water samples'
responses to fertilizer, what could account for those differences? Explain.

_____

_____

_____

_____

Connect **TO THE ESSENTIAL QUESTION**

12 **Applying Concepts** If a farmer uses too much fertilizer on a field, where
might the excess fertilizer end up? What are the possible consequences of this?

_____

_____

_____

_____

FIELD LAB INDEPENDENT *Inquiry*

Investigating Water Quality

In this lab you will collect samples of water from various locations and compare their chemical and biological properties. Then you will conduct a test to see how each sample changes over time after adding a small amount of garden fertilizer.

    Use caution when collecting water samples from a natural source such as a lake, river, or pond. If you cannot swim, ask an adult to collect the samples for you. Use care to avoid harmful plants around water sources.

PROCEDURE

ASK A QUESTION

1 In this lab, you will investigate the following questions: How does the quality of water vary from different sources? How does fertilizer runoff affect water quality?

DEVELOP A PLAN

2 Work with your partner to decide what sources of water you will include in your survey of water quality. Be sure that you include at least two natural sources and two sources that are either commercial or treated by humans. Write your plan below for each source of water that you plan to survey.

_____

_____

_____

_____

_____

_____

_____

_____

OBJECTIVES
• Survey the quality of water taken from a variety of sources.
• Investigate the effects of adding garden fertilizer to different water samples.

MATERIALS

For each pair
- bottles (4)
- cups, clear plastic
- garden fertilizer
- marker
- measuring spoons
- pH meter or pH paper
- water samples

For each student
- lab apron
- safety goggles

Field Lab continued

3 Work with your partner to decide how you will determine the quality of your samples. Decide what properties of water you will test using the provided equipment and materials. Set up a table to show the data you will collect and the samples you will survey.

4 Finally, make a plan for testing the response of each of your water samples to added fertilizer. Decide on a specific quantity of water and fertilizer to mix together as well as the conditions under which you will place these samples and the frequency with which you will observe them. Plan to observe them at regular intervals over a period of three weeks. Write out your plan in the form of a flowchart and then prepare a data table to show your data collection plan.

5 Obtain your teacher's approval for your plans.

MAKE OBSERVATIONS

6 Collect your water samples and carry out your plan for completing the water quality survey.

7 Carry out your plan for investigating the effects of fertilizer on your water samples.

Field Lab continued

ANALYZE THE RESULTS

8 **Comparing Samples** What results did you obtain as a result of your survey of water quality? Did you observe any differences in the water samples? Did the clarity, pH, or odor differ among the water samples you studied?

_____

_____

_____

_____

9 **Analyzing Observations** What results did you obtain from the experiment in which you added fertilizer to the water samples? Did the different samples all undergo the same changes in response to the fertilizer or did some change more than others?

DRAW CONCLUSIONS

10 **Comparing Results** If you observed differences in the water samples during your initial survey, what could account for those differences? Explain.

_____

_____

_____

_____

11 **Comparing Results** If you observed differences in the water samples' responses to fertilizer, what could account for those differences? Explain.

_____

_____

_____

_____

Connect TO THE ESSENTIAL QUESTION

12 **Applying Concepts** If a farmer uses too much fertilizer on a field, where might the excess fertilizer end up? What are the possible consequences of this?

_____

_____

_____

_____

Investigating Human Impact on the Land GENERAL

🏿 Small groups

🕐 30 minutes

MATERIALS

For each group

- online news articles related to local land issues

LAB RATINGS

LESS ←————————→ MORE

Teacher Prep —

Student Setup —

Cleanup —

My Notes

_____

_____

_____

_____

_____

TEACHER NOTES

In this activity, students are introduced to the controversies over human impacts on the environment. Each student will read an article that their group selects from an approved online source. The selected article should talk about an issue that affects land use in your local community. It may be helpful to provide a list of approved websites, instruct students to choose a one-page article, and follow up to ensure that each group decides on an article in a timely manner. Within their groups, students will identify the problem, the stakeholders, and the various positions taken by stakeholders. Then they will each choose which side they wish to take and debate with other students taking opposing sides.

Tip This lab will help students understand debate over issues related to human impact on land.

Student Tip Think about how many different people are affected by the way land is used and how the issue you are reading about affects you personally.

Skills Focus Evaluating Issues, Defending Positions

MODIFICATION FOR GUIDED *Inquiry*

For the guided inquiry option, provide students with the materials to be used as the basis for a specific position in the debate.

Answer Key

2. Accept all reasonable answers.

3. Accept all reasonable answers. Be sure that students are thinking about more than the most obvious stakeholders when they answer this question.

4. Accept all reasonable answers.

6. Accept all reasonable answers.

7. Accept all reasonable answers.

8. Accept all reasonable answers.

9. Accept all reasonable answers.

10. Accept all reasonable answers.

11. Accept all reasonable answers. Students should show that they recognize that land use issues are difficult to resolve because there are usually many different people with different interests in the way that certain areas of land are used. It can be very difficult to have everyone be happy with one particular outcome and often there is no satisfactory resolution of problems involving land use.

QUICK LAB INDEPENDENT Inquiry

Investigating Human Impact on the Land

In this activity, you will read about an environmental issue related to land use in your local area. Then you will identify the problem, the people affected by the problem, and the various positions taken on the issue. Then you will take one side of the issue and debate it.

PROCEDURE

1 Use the approved online sources to find an article that discusses an issue involving land use in your local community. As a group, decide on one article that your group will work on. Obtain your teacher's approval of your choice.

2 Choose one or two members to read the article and then discuss it. Choose another group member to write a summary that can be presented as your argument in the debate.

_____

_____

_____

3 Who are the people affected by the problem? Think of everyone affected, not just the people mentioned in the article.

_____

_____

_____

4 According to the article, are there two or more groups of people (called stakeholders) who have opposing views on the problem? As a group, talk about the stakeholders to identify them and to explain each of their positions on the problem.

_____

_____

_____

_____

_____

_____

OBJECTIVE
• Understand the complexity of issues involving land degradation by humans.

MATERIALS
For each group
• online news articles related to local land issues

Quick Lab continued

5 Within your own group, divide into smaller groups to debate the various positions you identified in Step 4.

6 What position did you support in the debate?

_____

7 Why did you support that position?

_____

_____

_____

8 Was your position initially supported by the majority?

_____

9 Did your group persuade the opposing group of your position?

_____

10 Was your position finally supported by the majority?

_____

11 What conclusions do you draw about how easily issues involving land use can be resolved?

_____

_____

_____

QUICK LAB DIRECTED Inquiry

Roots and Erosion GENERAL

👥 Small groups

🕐 15 minutes

LAB RATINGS

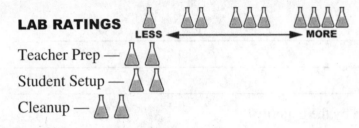

LESS ◄────────► MORE

Teacher Prep —

Student Setup —

Cleanup —

MATERIALS

For each group
- bowl, plastic (2)
- cup, clear plastic
- plants, potted, various
- soil, potting
- spoon, plastic
- water

For each student
- gloves
- lab apron
- safety goggles

SAFETY INFORMATION

Remind students to review all safety cautions and icons before beginning this lab. Water and soil on the floor can be a slipping hazard. Make sure all spills are cleaned up immediately. Remind students not to taste the plants, even if they are edible plants. Some students may have plant allergies; ask students about their allergies before selecting plants. Use bagged soil from a science supply house or garden center, rather than soil recovered from outside. Be sure to remind students to clean up carefully after the lab and to wash their hands thoroughly.

TEACHER NOTES

In this activity, students will observe how plant roots can prevent soil from eroding. Any type of seedling with extensive roots will work, such as basil or flowers that are sold in six-packs in plant nurseries. Loosen plants from their containers before giving them to students. For the soil-only test, students will need enough potting soil to fill the original plastic plant container. Before giving the potting soil to students, you may need to moisten it slightly to make it clump. Students should dispose of soil in a trash can, not by washing it down the sink.

Skills Focus Making Observations, Drawing Conclusions

MODIFICATION FOR INDEPENDENT Inquiry

Ask students to develop a simple procedure to test how plants affect soil erosion. Start by having students list variables related to plants that they think may affect soil erosion. Then, ask them to choose one variable to test. Guide students to focus on plant-related variables. Students should carry out all reasonable procedures and share their results with the class.

My Notes
_____
_____
_____
_____
_____

Answer Key

1. Sample answer: The roots form a network in the soil. They hold the soil in place and keep the shape of the pot.

2. Sample answer: The water is still pretty clear, but there are a few pieces of soil in it. Most of the soil is still around the roots of the plant.

4. Sample answer: The water is full of soil. The soil block fell apart.

5. Sample answer: Plants help prevent soil erosion because the roots help hold the soil in place.

6. Sample answer: Deforestation removes trees from the land. The tree roots help hold the soil in place. Without the roots, the soil will erode more easily.

QUICK LAB DIRECTED Inquiry

Roots and Erosion

In this activity, you will investigate how plants affect soil erosion. Soil erosion can lead to the loss of topsoil and to desertification. The Dust Bowl in the United States was caused by soil erosion in the Great Plains. Soil erosion continues to be a problem in many places in the world.

PROCEDURE

1 Gently remove the **plant** from its pot. The soil and roots should come out with the plant. Observe the roots and the soil. What do you notice?

_____

_____

_____

_____

_____

OBJECTIVES
- Describe how plant roots affect soil erosion.

MATERIALS

For each group
- bowl, plastic (2)
- cup, clear plastic
- plants, potted, various
- soil, potting
- spoon, plastic
- water

For each student
- gloves
- lab apron
- safety goggles

2 Put the plant in a **bowl**. Using the **cup**, slowly pour about one-half cup of **water** over the roots and soil. Describe the water in the bowl and the soil around the roots.

_____

_____

_____

_____

_____

3 Use the **spoon** to pack the plant pot with **potting soil.** Turn the pot upside down into the second bowl. Gently squeeze out the block of soil into the bowl.

Quick Lab continued

4 Slowly pour about one-half cup of water over the soil block. Describe the soil block and the water in the bowl.

_____

_____

_____

_____

_____

_____

_____

_____

5 Based on your observations, how do plants affect erosion?

_____

_____

_____

_____

_____

_____

_____

_____

6 Deforestation can lead to soil erosion. Explain why this happens.

_____

_____

_____

_____

_____

_____

_____

_____

_____

QUICK LAB DIRECTED Inquiry

Collecting Air-Pollution Particles GENERAL

👥 Student pairs

⏱ 10 minutes/day for 2 days

LAB RATINGS

LESS ⟵——————⟶ MORE

Teacher Prep —

Student Setup —

Cleanup —

MATERIALS

For each pair
- hole punch
- index cards,
  5 in. × 7 in. (10)
- magnifying lens
- petroleum jelly
- plastic spoon or
  paintbrush
- pushpins (10)
- string
- tape

For each student
- safety goggles

SAFETY INFORMATION

Remind students to review all safety cautions and icons before beginning this lab. Remind students to use caution when using pushpins.

TEACHER NOTES

In this activity, students will collect particulates to study the types of air pollution around your school.

Student Tip Be careful not to use too much petroleum jelly. You only need enough to cover the surface of the index card.

Skills Focus Collecting Data, Forming Hypotheses

MODIFICATION FOR INDEPENDENT Inquiry

Have students work in small groups to research the relationship between airborne particulates and air pollution. The group should work together to formulate a testable question or explanation based on their research. Next, the group will conduct a fair test to answer their question or support their explanation. Finally, the groups will communicate the procedures and results of their investigations through oral presentations.

My Notes

_____

_____

_____

_____

_____

Answer Key

5. Students' observations may vary.

6. Students' observations may vary. However, cards placed in or near high-traffic areas and directly under trees are likely to have the highest number of particles.

7. Students' observations may vary.

8. Sample answer: I found particles of pollen from the dogwood trees near the football field.

9. Students might hypothesize that automobile traffic contributes a large amount of particulate matter to the air. During certain times of the year, trees will also contribute significant particulates.

QUICK LAB DIRECTED *Inquiry*

Collecting Air-Pollution Particles

Is there pollution where you live? In this lab you will collect air-pollution particles from different locations.

PROCEDURE

1 Choose ten locations around your school and label each **index card.**

2 Use a **plastic spoon** or a small **paintbrush** to cover each index card with a thin coat of **petroleum jelly.**

3 Use a **pushpin** or **tape** to hang the cards around your school.

4 One day later, use a **magnifying lens** to count the number of particles on the cards. Record your particle totals in the data table below.

OBJECTIVE
- Collect and analyze air pollution particulates.

MATERIALS
For each pair
- hole punch
- index cards, 5 in. × 7 in. (10)
- magnifying lens
- petroleum jelly
- plastic spoon or paintbrush
- pushpins (10)
- string
- tape

For each student
- safety goggles

PARTICLE TOTALS

Location of card										
Number of particles										

5 Which location had the fewest particles? _____

6 Which location had the most particles? _____

7 Is there more than one type of particle? _____

Quick Lab continued

8 Can you identify the particles and their sources?

_____

_____

_____

_____

_____

_____

_____

9 Hypothesize why some locations had more particles than other locations.

_____

_____

_____

_____

_____

_____

_____

QUICK LAB DIRECTED Inquiry

Identifying Sources of Indoor Air Pollution GENERAL

👥 Small groups
🕐 30 minutes

MATERIALS

For each group
• digital camera
• paper
• pencils
• reference materials

LAB RATINGS LESS ⟵⟶ MORE

Teacher Prep —

Student Setup —

Cleanup —

My Notes

_____

_____

_____

_____

_____

TEACHER NOTES

In this activity, students will investigate the causes of indoor air pollution and brainstorm ways to reduce or eliminate it. They will then use their findings to create an informational brochure. The Environmental Protection Agency has on-line resources for teaching indoor air quality. Use the following keyword search in your favorite browser: EPA indoor air quality tools for schools.

Tip This activity may help students better understand how human actions impact the environment and how pollution affects them and their health.

Skills Focus Conducting Research, Making Observations, Communicating Results

MODIFICATION FOR GUIDED Inquiry

Ask student groups what they think the causes of indoor air pollution are and how air pollution affects their health. Have students determine a way to educate other students about indoor air pollution. Once you have read and approved the group's plan, have them carry it out. Remind students to record their sources while researching the topic.

Tip For students who are stuck, suggest one or more of the following: create a home walk-through checklist, design a pollutant flowchart, use a computer program to create a digital presentation, write and record an infomercial, or design and create informative posters.

MODIFICATION FOR INDEPENDENT Inquiry

Have each student group identify a question relating to air pollution. Each group should make a hypothesis and write a proposed procedure to test the hypothesis. Allow students to carry out any reasonable procedures. Have student groups present their findings.

Answer Key

1. Accept all reasonable answers.

2. **Teacher Prompt** Have groups determine beforehand where they are going to look for sources of indoor air pollution. They should divide places and tasks. If you cannot provide students with digital cameras, have them draw pictures.

3. Accept all reasonable answers.

4. Accept all reasonable answers.

5. Accept all reasonable brochures.

Identifying Sources of Indoor Air Pollution

In this activity, you will identify the causes of indoor air pollution. You will research causes of indoor air pollution and create a brochure to educate students about how to reduce it.

PROCEDURE

1 Use **research materials** to find the causes of indoor air pollution. Record your data and your sources in the spaces below.

_____

_____

_____

_____

_____

2 With your group, locate sources of indoor air pollution in your school. Use a **digital camera** to take pictures of the pollution sources. If you do not have a camera, draw pictures.

3 In the table below, record each source of indoor air pollution that you identified. Record whether the hazard type is physical, chemical, or biological. Record whether the exposure is the result of inhalation, ingestion, or skin contact. Consult your data to record some possible symptoms.

Source of indoor air pollution	Type of hazard	Exposure	Possible symptoms

OBJECTIVES

- Identify sources of indoor air pollution.
- Communicate ways to reduce or eliminate indoor air pollution.

MATERIALS

For each group
- digital camera
- paper
- pencils
- reference materials

Quick Lab continued

4 Brainstorm ways to reduce indoor air pollution.

_____

_____

_____

_____

_____

5 Work with your group to create an educational brochure teaching other students about what causes indoor air pollution and how to reduce it. Use the space below to sketch a plan of your brochure. Illustrate your brochure with your photographs or sketches. Share your completed brochures with the other groups.

QUICK LAB DIRECTED **Inquiry**

Soil Erosion GENERAL

👥 Small groups

🕐 30 minutes

LAB RATINGS

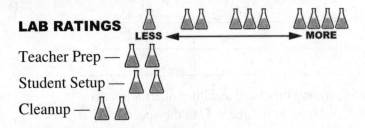

LESS ◄————————► MORE

Teacher Prep —

Student Setup —

Cleanup —

MATERIALS

For each group
- basin, large
- books (2)
- bottle caps (3 or 4)
- potting soil
- protractor
- sod
- water (2 L)
- watering can

For each student
- gloves
- lab apron
- safety goggles

SAFETY INFORMATION

Remind students to review all safety cautions and icons before beginning this lab. Students should wear protective gloves when handling soil and should wash their hands after handling soil. Water on the floor presents a slipping hazard. Students should report all spills immediately. Paper towels should be available to clean up spills.

TEACHER NOTES

In this activity, students will model the effects of using different methods to prevent soil erosion. They will observe the differences in the amount of erosion in loosely packed soil, densely packed soil, and reinforced and protected soil. You will need to gather potting soil, sod, and bottle caps prior to the activity period. The amount of potting soil required will depend on the size of the basins and the number of student groups, but one standard-size bag should be sufficient. If basins are unavailable, disposable baking sheets may be used. Students will have to place soil in the sheets before propping them on the books to prevent the sheets from bending or collapsing.

Have a large basin or trash can available for students to dispose of wet soil between tests. Water may be poured down the drain, provided it isn't too dirty. Water with too much soil in it may clog drains.

Skills Focus Making Models, Drawing Conclusions

My Notes

_____

_____

_____

_____

_____

MODIFICATION FOR GUIDED **Inquiry**

Ask students to design an experiment to test which has a greater effect on soil erosion: regular light rains or infrequent heavy rains. Have students propose a procedure, including all materials. They should create a plan for data collection and decide how they will analyze their data. They should present their data and conclusions in a lab report.

Quick Lab continued

MODIFICATION FOR INDEPENDENT Inquiry

Have students design an investigation to study a specific factor that may or may not affect erosion rates. They should create a plan for data collection and decide how they will analyze their data. They should present their data and conclusions to the class using a method of their choice.

Answer Key

3. Answers may vary, but students should notice that the water erodes a lot of soil. **Teacher Prompt** Is there soil in the water that collects at the bottom of the basin? How much soil is left where you placed it at the top of the basin? Sample answer: Yes, there is soil in the water. Most of the soil is still at the top of the basin.

6. Answers may vary, but students should notice that less soil is eroded than was eroded in the previous trial.

8. Answers may vary, but students should notice that the soil that is eroded from the top of the basin gets trapped and held by the bottle caps.

10. Answers may vary, but students should notice that the sod protects most of the soil from eroding.

11. Answers may vary. In general, planting vegetation will reduce soil erosion most effectively. Compacting soil will reduce erosion some, and embedding objects will prevent eroded soil from being completely removed.

12. Sample answers: Reducing soil erosion is beneficial because it reduces sediment in water bodies and helps preserve soil for agriculture and ecosystem development. Planting vegetation might introduce non-native species into an area. Compacting soil can increase runoff, which can carry pollution into water bodies. Embedding objects in the soil can be expensive, and the objects might eventually erode away and cause damage.

QUICK LAB DIRECTED Inquiry

Soil Erosion

In this lab, you will build a model of a hillside to explore different methods for reducing soil erosion. You will use a basin of potting soil set at an angle to represent the hillside, and a watering can to represent rain.

PROCEDURE

1 While wearing **gloves**, place enough **potting soil** in a **basin** to cover the upper 1/3 of the basin with a layer of soil about 2 cm thick.

2 Place the basin on top of **two books** so that the basin rests at about a 30° angle.

3 Use a **watering can** to sprinkle about 500 mL of **water** over the soil surface to simulate rain. Observe what happens to the soil, and record your observations.

_____

_____

_____

_____

_____

_____

4 Remove the soil and water from the basin. Use proper disposal methods as instructed by your teacher. Then, repeat Step 1.

5 Press on the soil surface to compact the soil as much as possible. If the soil does not compact easily, add a small amount of water to slightly moisten the soil and make it easier to compress. Prop the basin on top of the books again.

6 Repeat Steps 3 and 4.

_____

_____

_____

_____

_____

OBJECTIVES

- Model different methods for reducing soil erosion.
- Identify the most effective methods of preventing soil erosion.

MATERIALS

For each group
- basin, large
- books (2)
- bottle caps
- potting soil
- protractor
- sod
- water (2 L)
- watering can

For each student
- gloves
- lab apron
- safety goggles

Quick Lab continued

7 Repeat Steps 1 and 2, but push a few **bottle caps** into the soil about halfway down the slope.

8 Repeat Steps 3 and 4.

_____

_____

_____

_____

9 Repeat Steps 1 and 2, but place a layer of **sod** over the surface of the soil.

10 Repeat Step 3.

_____

_____

_____

_____

11 Which method reduced soil erosion the most: compacting the soil, embedding objects in the soil, or planting vegetation?

_____

_____

_____

_____

12 What are some advantages to reducing soil erosion? What are some disadvantages of using each of the erosion prevention methods you studied in this lab?

_____

_____

_____

_____

_____

QUICK LAB DIRECTED Inquiry

Investigate the Value
of Recycling GENERAL

👥 Student pairs
🕐 30 minutes

LAB RATINGS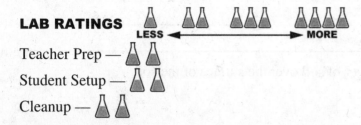

Teacher Prep —

Student Setup —

Cleanup —

MATERIALS

For each pair
- cups, plastic (2)
- die
- individually wrapped items (about 50) in a bag
- stopwatch or timer

My Notes

_____

_____

_____

_____

_____

TEACHER NOTES

In this activity, students are asked to evaluate the benefit of recycling through their experience with a model. In the model, students are asked to minimize the number of wrappers placed in a cup that represents a landfill. A second cup represents a recycling plant. Label each cup to avoid mistaking one for the other. To run the model, students roll a die. The outcome of the roll tells them what to do with the wrapper of an item they remove from a bag. For results 1 through 3, the item is unwrapped and the wrapper is placed in the cup representing the landfill. For results 4 through 6, the item is not unwrapped but is placed in the other cup. The outcome of each roll is recorded. After one minute, the student measures how much of the landfill cup is filled. The number of rolls ending with recycling is compared to the number of rolls that result in a wrapper going to the landfill. This procedure is repeated three times. Comparing the results from all four trials will show that the landfill cup fills up faster if there are more recycling events.

The items that you use for this activity could be any small objects that are wrapped in packaging that can be easily removed by students. Example items are individually wrapped toothpicks, adhesive bandages, or flossing picks.

Tip This lab will help students understand the benefits of recycling.

Skills Focus Developing Models, Drawing Conclusions

MODIFICATION FOR GUIDED Inquiry

For the Guided Inquiry option, have students plan their own model and run it after you have approved their plan.

Answer Key

5. Sample answer:

RESULTS OF WRAPPER DISPOSAL

Roll #	Number on die (1 to 6)	Item recycled? (y/n)	Roll #	Number on die (1 to 6)	Item recycled? (y/n)
1	2	n	13	2	n
2	3	n	14	5	y
3	6	y	15	1	n
4	3	n	16	6	y
5	1	n	17	Landfill full	Landfill full
6	4	y	18		
7	2	n	19		
8	5	y	20		
9	1	n	21		
10	6	y	22		
11	3	n	23		
12	5	y	24		

6. Sample answer:

SUMMARY OF WRAPPER DISPOSAL RESULTS

Trial	Number of recycling events	Number of landfill events	Time taken to fill landfill cup (m:s)
1	10	15	1:45
2	7	15	1:20
3	11	15	1:50
4	18	15	2:10

7. Sample answer: The landfill took longer to fill when there were more recycling events.

QUICK LAB DIRECTED *Inquiry*

Investigate the Value of Recycling

In this lab you will investigate how recycling affects the rate at which landfills are filled.

PROCEDURE

1 Mark one cup as the landfill and the other cup as the recycling center.

2 Start the model by taking a wrapped item from the bag.

3 Roll the die.

4 If the number on the die is 1, 2, or 3, unwrap the item and place the wrapper in the cup representing the landfill. If the result is 4, 5, or 6, place the wrapped item in the cup representing the recycling center. Record the outcome of each roll in the table provided.

OBJECTIVE

• Investigate how recycling slows the speed at which landfills are filled.

MATERIALS

For each pair
• cups, plastic (2)
• die
• individually wrapped items (about 50) in a bag
• stopwatch or timer

RESULTS OF WRAPPER DISPOSAL

Roll #	Number on die (1 to 6)	Item recycled? (y/n)	Roll #	Number on die (1 to 6)	Item recycled? (y/n)
1			13		
2			14		
3			15		
4			16		
5			17		
6			18		
7			19		
8			20		
9			21		
10			22		
11			23		
12			24		

Quick Lab continued

5 Repeat Steps 2–4 until the landfill cup is filled. Stop the timer! Record the time. Summarize your data in the table below.

SUMMARY OF WRAPPER DISPOSAL RESULTS

Trial	Number of recycling events	Number of landfill events	Time taken to fill landfill cup
1			
2			
3			
4			

6 Repeat Steps 2–5 for three more trials.

7 Compare the results of the four trials. In which case did the landfill fill fastest? Was there any trend based on how much recycling occurred compared to how much waste was sent to the landfill? Did you see any pattern emerge from the data?

_____

_____

_____

EXPLORATION LAB DIRECTED Inquiry AND GUIDED Inquiry

Filtering Water GENERAL

🫱 Small groups

⏱ 45 minutes

LAB RATINGS

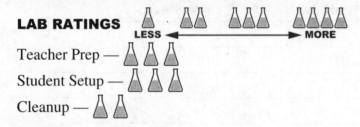

LESS ⟷ MORE

Teacher Prep —

Student Setup —

Cleanup —

SAFETY INFORMATION

Remind students to review all safety cautions and icons before beginning this lab. Sand and gravel can cause eye injuries, so students should wear goggles at all times. Water can present a slipping hazard, so all spills should be cleaned up immediately.

TEACHER NOTES

In this activity, students will design, build, and test a water filtration system to clean muddy water. The planning and design phases of the guided inquiry version of this investigation may require more time than the actual testing of the filters. You may want to have students build and test their filtration units in class and then answer questions as homework.

Each group will need the following earth materials: 1 L water mixed with 50 g soil; up to 500 mL pebbles; a 1 L bottle with the bottom cut off and a hole punched in the cap (can be done with a nail); up to 500 mL sand; and up to 500 mL soil. To reduce time, you will need to prepare the plastic bottles and muddy water before the activity period. To clean up after the activity, students should dump solid materials in the trash, not the sink. Dirty water may be poured down the sink.

This lab could also be performed with water containing various food products, such as coffee grounds, ketchup, mustard, pepper, and soy sauce. This gives students the opportunity to see that filtration will remove the solids but not the color or smell.

Tip This activity may help students better understand how groundwater is naturally filtered as it percolates through the ground.

Skills Focus Constructing Models, Analyzing Results

MATERIALS

For each group
- cotton balls (3)
- graduated cylinder, 100 mL
- muddy water
- pebbles
- plastic bottle, 1 L
- plastic cup
- sand
- small ring and stand
- soil

For each student
- gloves
- lab apron
- safety goggles

My Notes
_____
_____
_____
_____
_____

Exploration Lab continued

MODIFICATION FOR INDEPENDENT Inquiry

Explain to students that sometimes charcoal is used to filter water in commercial water filters. Ask students to research what types of natural materials can be used to filter water. Students should research and design their own water filtration systems. They should present a procedure, including a description and labeled sketch of their filtration unit, as well as a list of steps they will follow to filter water, record observations and data, and report conclusions. With teacher approval of their design and procedure, students should carry out their investigation and present their results in a lab report.

Answer Key for DIRECTED Inquiry

FORM A PREDICTION

2. Sample answer: Soil and sand are fine-grained and can be packed together. Pebbles have a lot of space between them. Cotton is superfine and would probably make a great filter.

3. Sample answer: The different materials could be layered on top of one another so that the pebbles filter out large solids and the sand, soil, and cotton filter out the smaller solids.

MAKE OBSERVATIONS

4. Sample answer: The water passed through the filter quickly at first, then more slowly. The larger solid particles were filtered out by the pebbles, and the sand, soil, and cotton filtered the smaller particles. I can see them through the side of the bottle. The water in the cup is still brown, but it does not have any large solids in it anymore.

ANALYZE THE RESULTS

7. Sample answer: Our filtered water looked dirtier than the tap water, but our filtered water looked cleaner than the muddy water we put into our filtration system. We should compare it to tap water because tap water acts as the control group for clean water.

8. Sample answer: The larger materials trapped the large solids in the muddy water, and the finer materials filtered the smaller solids. The order of the layering allowed the water to move more quickly through the filter because the spaces between the pebbles allowed most of the water to easily flow through to the bottom of the filter.

DRAW CONCLUSIONS

9. Sample answer: The way water flowed through our filtration system might be similar to the way water flows through sand and gravel as it becomes groundwater.

10. Sample answer: Freshwater quality might be improved if the water flows through an area that has a lot of dirt, sand, and pebbles.

Exploration Lab continued

Connect TO THE ESSENTIAL QUESTION

11. Sample answer: If people build a lot of roads and buildings and dig up the ground, then there won't be a way for water to filter through the ground and get cleaned.

Answer Key for GUIDED Inquiry

FORM A PREDICTION

2. Sample answer: Soil and sand are fine-grained and can be packed together. Pebbles have a lot of space between them. Cotton is superfine and would probably make a great filter.

3. Sample answer: The different materials could be layered on top of one another so that the pebbles filter out large solids and the sand, soil, and cotton filter out the smaller solids.

DEVELOP A PLAN

4. Sample answer: Student sketches will vary but should incorporate the plastic bottle, ring stand, and earth materials. Sketches should show the bottle overturned and set in ring stand, with layers of materials in the neck of the bottle. Designs should include labels for each part and each layer of material.

5. Sample answer: 1. Place water filtration unit in ring stand. Use hands to support filtration unit if necessary. 2. Place plastic cup under bottle cap. 3. Pour 200 mL of dirty water into open top of filtration unit. 3. Observe water filtration, including time it takes for water to pass through system.

MAKE OBSERVATIONS

7. Sample answer: The water took about five minutes to pass through the filtration unit. The water in the cup was still dirty, but much cleaner than when it was poured into the filtration unit. The larger solids have all been filtered out.

ANALYZE THE RESULTS

8. Answers will vary.

9. Sample answer: Our filtered water looked dirtier than the tap water, but our filtered water looked cleaner than the muddy water we put into our filtration system. We should compare it to tap water because tap water acts as the control group for clean water.

10. Sample answer: We used too many pebbles and not enough cotton balls. I would redesign the filtration unit using more cotton balls and sand to filter out the smaller solids, and fewer pebbles.

11. Sample answer: We used too much water, and it took too long to pass through the filter. I would change the procedure to indicate exactly how much water to use.

DRAW CONCLUSIONS

12. Sample answer: The best filters usually have layers of earth materials, with the finer materials near the bottom.

13. Sample answer: The way water flowed through our filtration system might be similar to the way water flows through sand and gravel as it becomes groundwater.

14. Sample answer: Freshwater quality might be improved if the water flows through an area that has a lot of dirt, sand, and pebbles.

Connect **TO THE ESSENTIAL QUESTION**

15. Sample answer: If people build a lot of roads and buildings and dig up the ground, then there won't be a way for water to filter through the ground and get cleaned.

EXPLORATION LAB DIRECTED *Inquiry*

Filtering Water

In this lab, you will build and test a water filtration system. You will use your water filtration system to clean muddy water using various earth materials. You will investigate which materials filter water more effectively and efficiently.

PROCEDURE

ASK A QUESTION

❶ In this lab, you will investigate the following question: How can you use common earth materials such as soil, sand, and pebbles to clean dirty water?

FORM A PREDICTION

❷ Examine the samples of earth materials provided by your teacher. Record your observations.

_____

_____

❸ Based on your observations, form a prediction as to how earth materials might be used to make muddy water cleaner.

_____

_____

MAKE OBSERVATIONS

❹ Place the **plastic bottle** upside down in the **ring stand.** Place a **plastic cup** beneath the perforated bottle cap.

❺ Put up to 500 mL of the different earth materials into the bottom of the bottle in the following order: **cotton balls**, **soil**, **sand**, and **pebbles** (pebbles should be the top layer).

OBJECTIVES

- Describe the way earth materials filter water.
- Model groundwater filtration.

MATERIALS

For each group
- cotton balls (3)
- graduated cylinder, 100 mL
- muddy water
- pebbles
- plastic bottle, 1 L
- plastic cup
- sand
- small ring and stand
- soil

For each student
- gloves
- lab apron
- safety goggles

Exploration Lab continued

6 Using the **graduated cylinder**, carefully pour 200 mL of **muddy water** into your water filtration unit. Observe the water percolating through the earth materials and accumulating in the cup. Record your observations.

_____

_____

_____

_____

_____

_____

_____

ANALYZE THE RESULTS

7 **Comparing Results** How does your filtered water compare to tap water? Why should you compare your results with tap water?

_____

_____

_____

_____

_____

_____

8 **Evaluating Models** Evaluate your water filtration system. What features of its design helped it to filter the muddy water?

_____

_____

_____

_____

_____

_____

_____

Exploration Lab continued

DRAW CONCLUSIONS

9 **Analyzing Models** How is the use of your filtration system similar to the cycle of freshwater on Earth?

_____

_____

_____

_____

_____

_____

10 **Interpreting Observations** What does your filtration system demonstrate about one way in which the quality of freshwater can be improved in a natural setting?

_____

_____

_____

_____

_____

_____

_____

Connect TO THE ESSENTIAL QUESTION

11 **Applying Concepts** What is one way that humans can have an impact on the way water is naturally filtered in the environment?

_____

_____

_____

_____

_____

_____

_____

EXPLORATION LAB GUIDED *Inquiry*

Filtering Water

In this lab, you will design, build, and test a water filtration system. You will use your water filtration system to clean muddy water using various earth materials. You will investigate which materials filter water more effectively and efficiently.

PROCEDURE

ASK A QUESTION

1 In this lab, you will investigate the following question: How can you use common earth materials such as soil, sand, and pebbles to clean dirty water?

FORM A PREDICTION

2 Examine the samples of earth materials provided by your teacher. Record your observations.

_____

_____

_____

_____

3 Based on your observations, form a prediction as to how earth materials might be used to make muddy water cleaner.

_____

_____

_____

_____

_____

_____

OBJECTIVES

• Describe the way earth materials filter water.

• Model groundwater filtration.

MATERIALS

For each group
• cotton balls (3)
• graduated cylinder, 100 mL
• muddy water
• pebbles
• plastic bottle, 1 L
• plastic cup
• sand
• small ring and stand
• soil

For each student
• gloves
• lab apron
• safety goggles

Exploration Lab continued

DEVELOP A PLAN

4 Use the **materials** provided to design a filtration system that will clean muddy water. Make a sketch of your filtration system. Show your design to your teacher.

_____

_____

_____

_____

_____

5 When your teacher has approved your design, create a procedure for using your filtration system to clean muddy water. Write down the steps you will use to test your system.

_____

_____

_____

_____

_____

6 Show your proposed procedure to your teacher. When your teacher has approved your procedure, carry it out.

MAKE OBSERVATIONS

7 Follow your procedure to test your filtration system. Observe how well it cleans muddy water. Record your observations in the space below.

_____

_____

_____

_____

_____

_____

Exploration Lab continued

ANALYZE THE RESULTS

8 **Comparing Results** How do your results compare with others in the class?

_____
_____

9 **Comparing Results** How does your filtered water compare to tap water? Why should you compare your results with tap water?

_____
_____

10 **Evaluating Models** Evaluate your water filtration system. Did it clean the muddy water? If you rebuilt your filtration system, what improvements would you make? Why do you think these changes would help?

_____
_____
_____
_____
_____
_____
_____
_____

11 **Evaluating Methods** Evaluate your procedure. Did your method allow you to make the observations you needed to answer the questions? What steps would you add or remove to improve your procedure?

_____
_____
_____
_____
_____
_____
_____

Exploration Lab continued

DRAW CONCLUSIONS

⑫ Comparing Models Do the best filters have anything in common?

_____

_____

_____

_____

⑬ Analyzing Models How is the use of your filtration system similar to the cycle of freshwater on Earth?

_____

_____

_____

_____

⑭ Interpreting Observations What does your filtration system demonstrate about one way in which the quality of freshwater can be improved in a natural setting?

_____

_____

_____

_____

Connect TO THE ESSENTIAL QUESTION

⑮ Applying Concepts What is one way that humans can have an impact on the way water is naturally filtered in the environment?

_____

_____

_____

_____

_____